A Concise Introduction to E

In this short and very practical introduction to econometrics Philip Hans Franses guides the reader through the essential concepts of econometrics. Central to the book are practical questions in various economic disciplines, which can be answered using econometric methods and models. The book focuses on a limited number of the essential, most widely used methods, before going on to review the basics of econometrics. The book ends with a number of case studies drawn from recent empirical work to provide an intuitive illustration of what econometricians do when faced with practical questions. Throughout the book Franses emphasizes the importance of specification, evaluation, and implementation of models appropriate to the data.

Assuming basic familiarity only with matrix algebra and calculus, the book is designed to appeal as either a short stand-alone introduction for students embarking on an empirical research project or as a supplement to any standard introductory textbook.

PHILIP HANS FRANSES is Professor of Applied Econometrics and Professor of Marketing Research at Erasmus University, Rotterdam. He has published articles in leading journals and serves on a number of editorial boards, and has authored several textbooks, including *Non-Linear Time Series Models in Empirical Finance* (2001, with Dick van Dijk).

A Concise Introduction to Econometrics

An Intuitive Guide

— ‡ —

Philip Hans Franses

Econometric Institute,
Erasmus University, Rotterdam

CAMBRIDGE
UNIVERSITY PRESS

PUBLISHED BY THE PRESS SYNDICATE OF THE UNIVERSITY OF CAMBRIDGE
The Pitt Building, Trumpington Street, Cambridge CB2 1RP, United Kingdom

CAMBRIDGE UNIVERSITY PRESS
The Edinburgh Building, Cambridge, CB2 2RU, UK
40 West 20th Street, New York, NY 10011-4211, USA
477 Williamstown Road, Port Melbourne, VIC 3207, Australia
Ruiz de Alarcón 13, 28014 Madrid, Spain
Dock House, The Waterfront, Cape Town 8001, South Africa

http://www.cambridge.org

First published 2002

Printed in the United Kingdom at the University Press, Cambridge

Typefaces Meridien 10.5/16 pt and Stone Sans   *System* LaTeX 2_ε [TB]

A catalogue record for this book is available from the British Library

Library of Congress Cataloging in Publication data

Franses, Philip Hans, 1963–
A concise introduction to econometrics : an intuitive guide/Philip Hans Franses.
    p. cm.
Includes bibliographical references and index.
ISBN 0 521 81769 2 – ISBN 0 521 52090 8 (pb.)
1. Econometrics.   2. Econometrics – Case studies.   I. Title.
HB139 .F722   2002
330′.01′5195 – dc21   2002067380

ISBN 0 521 81769 2 hardback
ISBN 0 521 52090 8 paperback

Contents

Contents

Figures

Tables

Preface

This book is targeted at two distinct audiences. The first audience concerns novices in econometrics who consider taking an econometrics course in an advanced undergraduate or a graduate program. For them, this book aims to be an introduction to the field, and hopefully such that they do indeed take such courses. It should be stressed, though, that this is not a condescending book – that is, it is not something like "econometrics for dummies." On the contrary, the reader is taken seriously and hence some effort is required. The second audience consists of colleagues who teach these courses. It is my belief that many econometrics courses, by zooming in on theory and less on practice, are missing the most important aspect of econometrics, which is that it truly is a very practical discipline.

Therefore, central to this book are practical questions in various economic disciplines such as macroeconomics, finance, and marketing, which might be answered by using econometric tools. After a brief discussion of a few basic tools, I review various aspects of econometric modeling.

Along these lines, I also discuss matters which are typically skipped in currently available textbooks, but which are very relevant when one aims to apply econometric methods in practice. Next, several case studies should provide some intuition of what econometricians do when they face practical questions. Important concepts are shown in *italic* type; examples of practical questions which econometricians aim to answer will be shown in **bold** type.

This book might be used prior to any textbook on econometrics. It can, however, never replace one of these, as the discussion in this book is deliberately very sketchy. Also, at times this book has a somewhat polemic style, and this is done on purpose. In fact, this is the "personal twist" in this book. Therefore, the book should not be seen as the ultimate treatment of the topic, but merely as a (hopefully) joyful read before one takes or gives econometrics classes. Hence, the book can be viewed as a very lengthy introductory chapter.

Finally, as a way of examining whether a reader has appreciated the content of this book, one might think about the following exercise. Take a newspaper or a news magazine and look for articles on economic issues. In many articles are reports on decisions which have been made, forecasts that have been generated, and questions that have been answered. Take one of these articles, and then ask whether these decisions, forecasts, and answers could have been based on the outcomes of an econometric model. What kind of data could one have used? What could the model have looked like? Would one have great confidence in these outcomes, and how does this extend to the reported decisions, forecasts, and answers?

I wish to thank Clive Granger and Ashwin Rattan at Cambridge University Press, for encouragement and helpful comments. Also, many thanks are due to Martijn de Jong, Dick van Dijk, and in particular Christiaan Heij for their very constructive remarks. Further comments or suggestions are always welcome. The address for correspondence is Econometric Institute, Erasmus University Rotterdam, P.O. Box 1738, NL-3000 DR Rotterdam, The Netherlands, email: franses@few.eur.nl

PHILIP HANS FRANSES
Rotterdam

CHAPTER ONE

Introduction

I n this chapter I provide an introductory discussion of what econometrics is and what econometricians do. Next, I consider a more detailed motivation for writing this book. Finally, I give an outline of the other chapters of the book.

What is econometrics?

Econometric techniques are usually developed and employed for answering practical questions. As the first five letters of the word "econometrics" indicate, these questions tend to deal with economic issues, although applications to other disciplines are widespread. The economic issues can concern macroeconomics, international economics, and microeconomics, but also finance, marketing, and accounting. The questions usually aim at a better understanding of an actually observed phenomenon and sometimes also at providing forecasts for future situations. Often it is hoped that these insights can be used to modify current policies or to put forward new strategies. For example, one may wonder about the causes of economic crises, and if these are identified, one can think of trying to reduce the effects of crises in the future. Or, it may be interesting to know what motivates people to donate to charity, and use this in order to better address prospective donors. One can also try to understand how stock markets go up – and, particularly, how they go down – in order to adjust investment decisions.

The whole range of econometric methods is usually simply called "econometrics," and this will also be done in this book. And anyone who either invents new econometric techniques, or applies old or new techniques, is called an "econometrician." One might also think of an econometrician as being a statistician who investigates the properties particular to economic data. Econometrics can be divided into *econometric theory* and *applied econometrics*. Econometric theory usually involves the development of new methods and the study of their properties. Applied econometrics concerns the development and application of tools to solve relevant practical questions.

In order to answer practical questions, econometric techniques are applied to actually observed data. These data can concern (1) observations over time, like a country's GDP when measured annually, (2) observations across individuals, like donations to charity, or (3) observations over time and over individuals. Perhaps "individuals" would be better phrased as "individual cases," to indicate that these observations can also concern countries, firms, or households, to mention just a few. Additionally, when one thinks about observations over time, these can concern seconds, days, or years.

Sometimes the relevant data are easy to access. Financial data concerning, for example, stock markets, can be found in daily newspapers or on the internet. Macroeconomic data on imports, exports, consumption, and income are often available on a monthly basis. In both cases one may need to pay a statistical agency in order to be able to download macroeconomic and financial indicators. Data in marketing are less easy to obtain, and this can be owing to issues of confidentiality. In general, data on individual behavior are not easy and usually are costly to obtain, and often one has to survey individuals oneself.

As one might expect, the type of question that one intends to answer using an econometric method is closely linked to the availability of actual data. When one can obtain purchase behavior of various households, one can try to answer questions about this behavior. If there are almost no data, there is usually not much to say. For example, a question like **"how many households will use this new product within 10 years from now?"** seems rather difficult to answer. And, **"what would the stock market do next year?"** is complicated, too. Of course, one can always come up with an answer, but whether one would have great confidence in this answer is rather doubtful. This touches upon a key aspect of the application of econometric techniques, which is that one aims at answering questions with *some* *degree of confidence*. In other words, econometricians do not provide answers like "yes" or "no," but instead one will hear something like "with great confidence we believe that poor countries will not catch up with rich countries within the next 25 years." Usually, the size of "great" in "great confidence" is a choice, although a typical phrase would be something like "with 95 per cent confidence." What that means will become clear in chapter 2 below.

The econometrician uses an *econometric model*. This model usually amounts to one or more equations. In words, these equations can be like "the probability that an individual donates to charity is 0.6 when the same individual donated last time and 0.2 when s/he did not," or "on average, today's stock market return on the Amsterdam Exchange is equal to yesterday's return on the New York Stock Exchange," or "the upward trend in Nigeria's *per capita* GDP is half the size of that of Kenya." Even though these three examples are hypothetical, the verbal expressions come close to the outcomes of actual econometric models.

The key activities of econometricians can now be illustrated. First, an econometrician needs to *translate a practical question* like, for example, **"what can explain today's stock market returns in Amsterdam?"** *into a model*. This usually amounts to thinking about the economic issue at stake, and also about the availability and quality of the data. Fluctuations in the Dow Jones may lead to similar fluctuations in Amsterdam, and this is perhaps not much of a surprise. However, it is by no means certain that this is best observed for daily data. Indeed, perhaps one should focus only on the first few minutes of a trading day, or perhaps even look at monthly data to get rid of erratic and irrelevant fluctuations, thereby obtaining a better overall picture. In sum, a key activity is to translate a practical question into an econometric model, where this model also somehow matches with the available data. For this translation, econometricians tend to rely on mathematics, as a sort of language. Econometricians are by no means mathematicians, but mathematical tools usually serve to condense notation and simplify certain technical matters. First, it comes in handy to know a little bit about matrix algebra before taking econometrics courses. Note that in this book I will not use any such algebra as I will just stick to simple examples. Second, it is relevant to know some of the basics of calculus, in particular, differential and integral calculus. To become an econometrician, one needs to have some knowledge of these tools.

The second key activity of an econometrician concerns the *match of the model with the data*. In the examples above, one could note numerical statements such as "equal" or "half the size." How does one get these numbers? There are various methods to get them, and these are collected under the header "estimation." More precisely, these numbers are often associated with unknown parameters. The notion "parameter estimation" already indicates that econometricians are never certain about these numbers. However, what econometricians can do is to provide a certain degree of confidence around these numbers. For example, one could say that **"it is very likely that growth in *per capita* GDP in Nigeria is smaller than that of Kenya"** or that **"it is unlikely that an individual donates to charity again if s/he did last time."** To make such statements, econometricians use statistical techniques.

Finally, a third key activity concerns the *implementation of the model outcomes*. This may mean the construction of *forecasts*. It can also be possible to simulate the properties of the model and thereby examine the effects of various policy rules.

To summarize, econometricians use economic insights and mathematical language to construct their econometric model, and they use statistical techniques to analyze its properties. This combination of three input disciplines ensures that courses in econometrics are not the easiest ones to study.

In this book I try to introduce the essentials of econometrics to novices, keeping the mathematical and statistical level at a minimum, but without being condescending. This book can be used prior to any textbook on econometrics, but it should certainly not replace it! The intention is that this book should be used as introductory and supplementary reading. For textbooks on econometrics, one can choose from Verbeek (2000), Koop (2000), Gujarati (1999), Kennedy (1998), Ramanathan (1997), Johnston and Dinardo (1996), Griffiths, Hill and Judge (1993), and Goldberger (1991) at the introductory level, from Heij *et al.* (2002), Ruud (2000),

Greene (1999), Wooldridge (1999), and Poirier (1995), at the intermediate level, and from White (2000), Davidson and MacKinnon (1993), and Amemiya (1985), at the advanced level. For more specific analysis of time series, one can consider Franses (1998), Hamilton (1994), and Hendry (1995), and for financial econometrics, see Campbell, Lo and MacKinlay (1997).

So, do you have any interest in reading more about econometrics? If you are really a novice, then you can perhaps better skip the next section as this is mainly written for colleagues and more experienced econometricians. The final section is helpful, though, as it provides an outline of subsequent chapters.

Why this book?

Fellow econometricians may now wonder why I decided to write this book in the first place. Well, the motivation was based on my teaching experience at the Econometric Institute of the Erasmus University Rotterdam, where we teach econometrics at undergraduate level. My experience mainly concerns the empirical projects that undergraduate students have to do in their final year before graduation. For these projects, many students work as an intern, for example, with a bank or a consultancy firm, and they are supposed to answer a practical question which the supervising manager may have. Typically, this manager knows that econometricians can handle empirical data, and usually they claim to have available abundant data. Once the student starts working on the project, the following scenario is quite common. The manager appears not to have an exact question in mind, and the student ends up not only constructing an econometric model, but also precisely formulating the question. It is this combination that students find difficult, and indeed, a typical question I get is "how do I start?"

Observing this phenomenon, I became aware that many econometric textbooks behave as if the model is already given from the outset, and it seems to be suggested that the only thing an econometrician needs to do is to estimate the unknown parameters. Of course, there are many different models for different types of data, but this usually implies that textbooks contain a range of chapters treating parameter estimation in different models (see also Granger, 1994). Note that more recent textbooks also address the possibility that the model may be inappropriate and therefore these books contain discussions about diagnostic checks.

Of course, to address in a single textbook all the practical steps that one can take seems like an impossible enterprise. However, it should be possible to indicate various issues other than parameter estimation that arise when one wants to arrive at a useful econometric model. Therefore, in chapter 3 I will go through various concerns that econometricians have when they aim to answer a practical question. This is not to say that parameter estimation is unimportant.

I merely aim to convey that in practice there is usually no model to begin with!

Without wishing to go into philosophical discussions about econometrics, it seems fair to state that the notion of "a model given from the outset" dates back to the first developments in econometrics. In the old days (like, say, fifty years ago), econometricians were supposed to match (mainly macro-) economic theories to data, often with an explicit goal to substantiate the theory. In the unlucky event that the econometric model failed to provide evidence in favor of the theory, it was usually perceived that perhaps the data were wrong or the estimation method was incorrect, implying that the econometrician could start all over again.

A format of a typical econometrics textbook has its origin in this traditional view of econometrics. This view assumes that most aspects of a model, like the relevant variables, the way they are measured, the data themselves, and the functional form, are already available to the econometrician, and the only thing s/he needs to do is to fit the model to the data. The model components are usually assumed to originate from an (often macro-) economic theory, and there is great confidence in its validity. A consequence of this confidence is that if the data cannot be summarized by this model, the econometric textbook first advises us to consider alternative estimation techniques. Finally, and conditional upon a successful result, the resultant empirical econometric model is used to confirm (and perhaps in some cases, to disconfirm) the thoughts summarized in the economic theory. See Morgan (1990, 2002) for a detailed analysis of the development of econometric ideas.

There are several reasons why this traditional view is losing territory. The first is that there is a decreasing confidence in the usefulness of econometric models to confirm or disconfirm economic theories. Summers (1991) convincingly argues that important new macroeconomic insights can also be obtained from applying rather simple statistical techniques, and that the benefit of considering more complicated models is small. Granger (1999) gives a lucid illustration of the fact that the implications of even a simple economic theory are hard to verify.

With an increased application of econometric methods in finance and marketing, there also seems to be a need for teaching econometrics differently. The main reason for this need is that it is usually impossible to have strong prior thoughts about the model. Also, these modern application areas require new models, which are suggested by the data more than by a theory – see Engle (1995), Wansbeek and Wedel (1999), for example. Hence, an econometrician nowadays uses the data and other sources of information to construct the econometric model. With this stronger emphasis on the data, it becomes important to address in more detail the specification of a model, the evaluation of a model, and its implementation. The evaluation part is relevant for obtaining confidence in the outcomes. It is of course impossible to treat all these issues, and hence my decision to give a "guided tour."

Outline of the book

The remainder of this book consists of four chapters, of which the last merely presents a few recommendations.

Chapter 2 deals with a brief discussion of a few basic tools, and in fact it can be viewed as a very short overview of what a typical textbook in econometrics in part aims to tell. Most of the material in this chapter should be interpreted as discussing language and concepts.

As is common, I start with the linear regression model, which is the basic workhorse of an econometrician. Next, I discuss various matters of interest within the context of this model. I will try to explain these in plain English, at least if that is possible. To highlight important concepts, I will put them in *italic* type. Examples of practical questions which econometricians aim to answer will be highlighted in **bold** type.

Chapter 3 outlines most of the issues relevant for constructing an econometric model to answer a practical question. In this chapter I will try to indicate that parameter estimation, once the model is given and the data are available, amounts to only a relatively small fragment of the whole process. In fact, the process of translating a question into a model involves many important decisions, which together constitute the so-called "empirical cycle." Examples of these decisions concern the question itself, the data used, the choice of the model (as there are many possible options), the modification of the model in case things go wrong, and the use of the model.

In chapter 4, I will concisely review some econometric studies which have been published in international refereed journals. The fact that they have been published should be seen as some guarantee that the results and the used methods make sense, although one can never be certain. Additionally, these examples all originate from my own work with co-authors. This is not meant to say that these are the best examples around, but at least I can recall the motivations for various decisions. Also, no one gets hurt, except perhaps myself (and my co-authors, but they were apparently thrill-seekers anyway). The illustrations serve to show how and why decisions have been made in order to set up a model to match the relevant questions with the available data. The examples concern empirical work in macroeconomics, finance, and marketing, but also in political science and temperature forecasting.

— ✦ CHAPTER TWO ✦ —

A few basic tools

As with any scientific discipline, there is some nomenclature in econometrics that one should get familiar with
before one appreciates applications to practical problems.
This nomenclature mainly originates from statistics and
mathematics, although there are also some concepts that
are specific only to econometrics. Naturally, there are many
ways to define concepts and to assign meaning to words.
In this chapter I aim to provide some intuitively appealing
meanings, and of course, they are far from precise. Again,
this should not be seen as a problem, as the textbooks to be
consulted by the reader at a later stage will be much more
precise.

This chapter contains five sections. The first deals with
probability densities, which are key concepts in statistics. In
the second section, I will bring these concepts a few steps
closer to econometrics by discussing the notions of conditional and unconditional expectations. An unconditional
expectation would be that there is a 60 per cent chance
that tomorrow's Amsterdam stock return is positive, which

would be a sensible statement if this happens on average on sixty out of the 100 days. In contrast, a conditional expectation would be that tomorrow's Amsterdam stock market return will be positive with a 75 per cent chance, where today's closing return in New York was positive, too. In the third section, I will link the conditional expectation with samples and a data generating process, and treat parameter estimation and some of its related topics. I will also dedicate a few words to the degree of uncertainty in practice, thereby demonstrating that econometrics is not a discipline like physics or chemistry but that it comes much closer to psychology and sociology. Hence, even though econometrics at first sight looks like an engineering kind of discipline, it is far from that. In the fourth section I discuss a few practical considerations, which will be further developed in chapter 3. The last section summarizes.

Distributions

A key concept in econometrics is the *distribution* of the data. One needs data to be able to set up an econometric model to answer a practical question, and hence the properties of the data are of paramount importance. Various properties of the data can be summarized by a distribution, and some properties can be used to answer the question.

A good starting-point of practical econometric work is to think about the possible *distributional properties* of the data. When thinking about bankruptcies, there are only two possibilities, that is "yes" or "no," which is usually called a *binary* or *dichotomous* phenomenon. However, when thinking about brand choice, one usually can choose between more than two brands. Furthermore, if one thinks about dollar sales in retail stores, this *variable* can take values ranging from zero to, say, millions, with anything in between. Such a variable is continuous.

A frequently considered distribution is the *normal distribution*. This distribution seems to match with many phenomena in economics and in other sciences, and that explains both its popularity and its name. Of course, the normal distribution is just one example of a wide range of possible distributions. Its popularity is also due to its mathematical convenience. The histogram of this distribution takes a bell-shaped pattern, as in figure 2.1. This graph contains something like a continuous histogram for a variable z, as it might be viewed as connecting an infinite number of bars. The graph in figure 2.1 is based on the mathematical expression

$$\phi(z) = \frac{1}{\sqrt{2\pi}} e^{-\frac{1}{2}z^2}, \tag{2.1}$$

where z can take values ranging from minus infinity $(-\infty)$ to plus infinity $(+\infty)$, where e is the natural number (approximately equal to 2.718), and where π is about 3.142. The graph gives $\phi(z)$ on the vertical axis and z is on the horizontal axis. The expression itself is due to Carl Friedrich Gauss (1777–1855), who is one of the most famous German

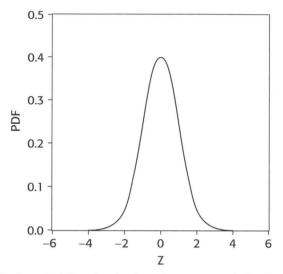

Figure 2.1 *A probability density function: a normal distribution*

scientists. For the moment, it is assumed that the mean of z is equal to zero and that its dispersion (variance) equals 1. The resultant distribution is called the *standard normal distribution*. When this is relaxed to a variable y with mean μ and variance σ^2, respectively, (2.1) becomes

$$\phi(y) = \frac{1}{\sigma\sqrt{2\pi}}e^{-\frac{1}{2}(\frac{y-\mu}{\sigma})^2}. \tag{2.2}$$

This expression is called the *probability density function (pdf)* for the variable y. From figure 2.1 and also from (2.2), one can see that this distribution is symmetric, as one takes squares of $\frac{y-\mu}{\sigma}$. To save notation, (2.2) is usually written as

$$y \sim N(\mu, \sigma^2), \tag{2.3}$$

where "~" means "is distributed as," and where "N" means "normal." In words, it says that a variable y has a normal distribution with mean μ and variance σ^2. By the way, σ is also called the *standard deviation*, which can be interpreted as a scaling measure.

The pdf allows one to see how many observations are in the middle, and hence close to the mean μ, and how many are in the tails. Obviously, as the pdf is reflected by a continuous histogram, one can understand that the area underneath the graph is equal to 1, which in words means that the sum of the probabilities of all possible outcomes is equal to 1. A more formal way of putting this is that

$$\int_{-\infty}^{+\infty} \frac{1}{\sqrt{2\pi}} e^{-\frac{1}{2}z^2} \, dz = 1. \tag{2.4}$$

If the histogram were to concern fixed intervals of z, like age categories, then (2.4) says that the sum of all fractions is equal to 1.

Sometimes it may be of interest to consider the total area underneath the pdf up to a certain point. This can be useful for statements like **"which fraction of stores has sales lower than 1,500 dollars?"** or **"which fraction of donors gives less than 30 dollars?"** Such an area is then equal to

$$\Phi(z) = \int_{-\infty}^{z} \frac{1}{\sqrt{2\pi}} e^{-\frac{1}{2}z^2} \, dz. \tag{2.5}$$

This is called the *cumulative density function (cdf)*. A graph of the cdf belonging to the pdf in figure 2.1 is given in figure 2.2.

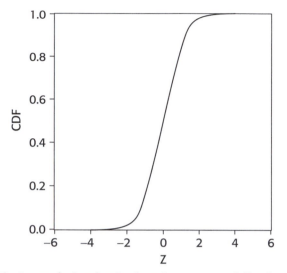

Figure 2.2 *A cumulative density function: a normal distribution*

In words, figure 2.2 says that, for example, almost all observations on a standard normal distribution are smaller than 4.

An example of a variable which might be distributed as normal is the total dollar sales in large retail stores, where it is assumed that sales close to zero are rare. Another case in which this distribution pops up concerns the shoe size of adult males or the exam scores (on a 1–100 scale) of graduate students.

In practice the mean μ is usually unknown and in fact one usually wants to get to know it. Suppose one is interested in the mean μ of the distribution of retail store sales. One can then consider a sample of n stores and compute the sample mean of observations on sales y_i, with $i = 1, 2, \ldots, n$, that is,

$$\hat{\mu} = \frac{y_1 + y_2 + \cdots + y_n}{n}, \tag{2.6}$$

where econometricians commonly use "hats" on Greek letters to indicate that an unknown parameter gets estimated.
When the sample data match with the normal distribution
with unknown mean μ, this $\hat{\mu}$ provides a reliable estimate
of its value. Such reliability is commonly associated with an
absence of a systematic bias, or with the notion of consistency, which involves that when n gets larger, $\hat{\mu}$ gets closer
and closer to μ. The estimated mean $\hat{\mu}$ can also be used to
make a prediction of what will be the most likely sales in a
previously unseen store or the shoe size of an adult male.
In other words, the mean can be used to quantify an *expectation*, an operator usually abbreviated as E. In many cases
one wants to evaluate the particular value of the mean, and
say something like "it is larger than expected," or "it is not
zero." In order to do that, one has to assume something
about the sample of observations, but I will return to this
below.

The linear regression model

In reality it rarely happens that observations in samples
are perfectly normally distributed. What does happen is
that, given that one corrects for certain aspects of the data,
one gets a normal distribution. For example, if one drew a

histogram of the size in centimeters of all individuals on the globe, one would not get a distribution like that in figure 2.1. In some parts of the world, people are shorter than elsewhere; children and adults typically differ in size and also males and females differ in height. However, it may well be that the distribution of the height of boys of age 12–14 in Northern European countries comes closer to a normal distribution.

Also, it is likely that total dollar sales are larger for larger stores. Suppose the average size of a store is, say, 500 square meters, and denote a variable x_i as the difference between the size of store i and this average size. Suppose further that store sales for an average sized store (say, in a week) are on average equal to 2,000 dollars, and label this as β_1. Additionally, stores which are larger than the average store sell more than those which are smaller, thereby not considering possible differences in prices, quality of personnel, and general atmosphere for the moment. Let this effect be equal to $\beta_2 = 2$. Taking this together, we have that the weekly sales in store i on average equals $y_i = 2000 + 2(x_i - 500)$ – that is, y_i depends in a linear way on x_i. In words, a store which is twice as large as an average store is expected to sell 3,000 dollars' worth of goods, while a store half the size of an average store sells only 1,500 dollars' worth.

This example about store sales brings us a step closer to what econometrics is all about. By making sales a function of store size, one might say something about the expected sales for a previously unseen store, when one knew its size.

Hence, if one opened a new store of 1,500 square meters, one might expect that weekly sales would be 4,000 dollars. Of course, it is unlikely that this would be precisely the outcome. However, it is the most likely value, given the assumed link between sales and store size. This link establishes a shift from the *unconditional expectation*, as discussed above, to the *conditional expectation*, which is of interest to econometricians. This latter concept is an example of what can be called a *model*.

To take this one step further, one might now believe that the sales variable, corrected for the effect of store size, is again normal. In other words, the *conditional distribution* of sales is normal. In this case, $y_i - 2000 - 2(x_i - 500)$, which of course equals $y_i - 1000 - 2x_i$, could be normally distributed. In many cases, the exact values 1,000 and 2, which appear here, are unknown and in practice one should estimate them. Hence, it is perhaps better to say that $y_i - \beta_1 - \beta_2 x_i$ is conditionally normal distributed, where β_1 and β_2 are unknown parameters. In mathematical notation, one then replaces

$$y_i \sim N(\mu, \sigma^2) \qquad (2.7)$$

from (2.3) by

$$y_i \sim N(\beta_1 + \beta_2 x_i, \sigma^2), \qquad (2.8)$$

that is, the unconditional mean μ gets replaced by the conditional mean $\beta_1 + \beta_2 x_i$. For a sample of store sales, together with their store sizes, one can now try to estimate β_1 and

β_2, as well as σ^2. Of course, this econometric model contains only one variable y_i and one variable x_i, and one can think of many other variables relevant to sales. For the purposes of this chapter, it does not matter much whether there is one such x_i or more, so for notational convenience, I stick to just this simple case.

Typically, one rewrites (2.8) by bringing the conditional expectation out of the parentheses, that is by considering $(y_i - \beta_1 - \beta_2 x_i) \sim N(0, \sigma^2)$, thereby getting

$$y_i = \beta_1 + \beta_2 x_i + \varepsilon_i, \tag{2.9}$$

where the variable ε_i by definition obeys

$$\varepsilon_i \sim N(0, \sigma^2). \tag{2.10}$$

These two equations constitute a key concept in econometrics (but also other disciplines), which is the so-called *linear regression model*. In this case, the model has a single *explanatory variable*, which is x_i. As we have said, one can extend (2.9) to have a lot more explanatory variables. The variable with effect β_1 is usually called the "constant term," as it does not involve x_i. The parameter β_1 itself is called the *intercept*. Furthermore, the model is a linear model. A nonlinear version of (2.9) could for example involve the variable x_i^δ.

To complete the nomenclature, at least for the moment, we need to mention that y_i is called the *dependent variable* or the *variable to be explained*. Another name for x_i is that it is an *independent variable*, as it does not in turn depend on y_i. For the ε_i variable there are many different names. First of all, it is important to note that β_1 and β_2 are unobserved and have to be estimated, and hence that ε_i cannot be observed and one can get only estimates of all its n values. These are rather useful, as the estimated values $\hat{\varepsilon}_i$ can be compared, for example, with the assumption of normality, in order to see if (2.10) amounts to an approximately valid assumption. From (2.10) it can be seen that the best forecast for ε_i equals 0. Hence, sometimes this variable is called an *innovation* as innovations by their very nature can not be forecasted. Another label for ε_i is that is represents an *error*. This word originates from the idea that for each pair of observations (y_i, x_i), their relation would be equal to $y_i = \beta_1 + \beta_2 x_i$, but this never holds exactly, simply because the probability that ε_i equals exactly zero given (2.10) is zero too! There may be a measurement error, or one may have forgotten to include a potentially relevant variable z_i. For the store sales example, this z_i could be the quality of store personnel. Related to the notion of an error is that of a *disturbance*. This name reflects the idea that there is some unknown variable which blurs our insight into the linear link between y_i and x_i. Finally, some textbooks call $\hat{\varepsilon}_i$ the *residual*. This notion of a residual can also be interpreted as that part of y_i which cannot be explained by a constant term and the explanatory variable x_i. It is always good to be aware of the fact that econometricians sometimes use different words for the same entity.

Inference

In order to assign some meaning to the properties of sample observations, one usually assumes that there is something like a *data generating process (DGP)*, which generates the sample data. Statisticians may call this the "population."

There are at least two things that one typically wants to do with sample data, when they are summarized in an econometric model. The first is to estimate key parameters of the (conditional) distribution of the observations, thereby again assuming that the DGP and the sample have the same properties. The second is that one wants to assign some confidence to these estimates. An exemplary statement is that "the mean of the observations is estimated to range from 3 to 5 with 90 per cent confidence." One may now wonder why one reads about percentages such as 90 per cent or 95 per cent. The key reason is that it implies that one might make a small mistake, with probability 10 per cent or 5 per cent. Indeed, the probability that the mean in the above example does not lie in between 3 and 5 is 10 per cent.

An econometric model contains *unknown parameters*. With the data and the model at hand, econometricians use *estimators* for these parameters, and their numerical outcomes are called *estimates*. An example of an estimator is

$$\hat{\mu} = \frac{y_1 + y_2 + \cdots + y_n}{n}, \tag{2.11}$$

which is an estimator of the unknown mean μ of the variable y. Whether this estimator is meaningful depends on the case at hand. Indeed, there are economic data for which an average value is not very interesting, as is the case for trending time series data. Another example of an estimator is

$$\hat{\sigma}^2 = \frac{(y_1 - \hat{\mu})^2 + (y_2 - \hat{\mu})^2 + \cdots + (y_n - \hat{\mu})^2}{n}, \quad (2.12)$$

which is called the *sample variance*.

A next thing to know concerns the reliability of $\hat{\mu}$ and $\hat{\sigma}^2$. It is then useful to consider the error (usually called *standard error* or *se*) of $\hat{\mu}$. Without giving a formal proof, I mention here that the standard error of $\hat{\mu}$, where the sample data originate from a normal distribution, is

$$se_{\hat{\mu}} = \frac{\hat{\sigma}}{\sqrt{n}}. \quad (2.13)$$

Additionally, and again without proof, it approximately holds in large samples that

$$\frac{\hat{\mu}}{se_{\hat{\mu}}} \sim N(0, 1), \quad (2.14)$$

where $N(0, 1)$ denotes the standard normal distribution, and where $\frac{\hat{\mu}}{se_{\hat{\mu}}}$ is called the *t*-ratio (-value) or *z*-score. The reason why one would want to have an estimator and its associated standard error is that one can now examine if the estimate equals zero with some confidence. If one looks again at the normal density in figure 2.1, it can be appreciated that about 95 per cent of the area underneath the line is within the range of -2 and 2. In other words, for a standard normal distribution one can say that with a probability of about

95 per cent one would draw a value which is in between -2 and 2. Hence, one can say that with 95 per cent confidence it holds that

$$-2 \leq \frac{\hat{\mu}}{se_{\hat{\mu}}} \leq 2. \tag{2.15}$$

This means that if one were to draw 10,000 samples from a standard normal distribution, and computed $\frac{\hat{\mu}}{se_{\hat{\mu}}}$ in each case, one would likely find that (2.15) holds for about 9,500 samples.

Ratios like $\frac{\hat{\mu}}{se_{\hat{\mu}}}$ are very interesting for the regression model in (2.8), in particular for the parameter β_2. Indeed, one may be interested in seeing whether $\hat{\beta}_2$ is equal to zero or not. If it is, one can conclude that x_i does not have explanatory value for y_i, which is sometimes defined as saying that x_i does not have an effect on y_i, which in our example means that store size would not explain store sales. Hence, one can make statements like "$\hat{\beta}_2$ is not equal to zero with 95 per cent confidence," or, "$\hat{\beta}_2$ differs from zero at the 5 per cent significance level." These statements allow for some uncertainty.

Going back to the purpose of answering practical questions, it is time to reconsider the above in the light of such questions. If one is interested in a question like **"does the level of yesterday's NYSE stock returns have an effect on the level of today's Amsterdam returns?"** one can consider a regression model like $y_t = \beta_1 + \beta_2 x_{t-1} + \varepsilon_t$, where y_t and x_t are daily returns in Amsterdam and in New York, respectively. The index t, $t = 1, 2, \ldots, T$ is usually used for time series data. Assuming a normal distribution, the question gets answered with a "yes," with confidence 95 per cent if $\hat{\beta}_2$ is not within the interval $[-2se_{\hat{\beta}_2}, +2se_{\hat{\beta}_2}]$ – or, put otherwise, if zero is not included in the interval $[\hat{\beta}_2 - 2se_{\hat{\beta}_2}, \hat{\beta}_2 + 2se_{\hat{\beta}_2}]$. In that case, one says that $\hat{\beta}_2$ is *significant at the 5 per cent* level, where again the 5 per cent combines with the value of 2.

Obviously, if one favored the so-called "efficient market hypothesis," which roughly says that stock returns cannot be forecast anyhow, one might zoom in on a statement of confidence that $\hat{\beta}_2$ is zero. For that matter, suppose one has found that $\frac{\hat{\beta}_2}{se_{\hat{\beta}_2}}$ equals 2.1, one might also conclude that the New York Stock Exchange (NYSE) returns do not have predictive value at the 1 per cent significance level. Interestingly, these conclusions can be drawn for the very same sample. It is perhaps this potentially confusing situation which make some people to say "lies, damn lies and statistics." Of course, it has nothing to do with lies, just with varying degrees of confidence.

The above example clearly demonstrates that there is room for subtleties when using statistical methods. This is not something one can prevent, but it just happens. Hence, when using econometric methods in practice, it seems wise to be as clear as possible on how one arrives at one's conclusion. In some cases it is perhaps better just to mention the value of $\hat{\beta}_2$ and its associated $se_{\hat{\beta}_2}$, and let the model user draw his or her own conclusions.

There are two further notions of relevance when estimating parameters. The first is that one usually wants to have an estimator that delivers what it promises to deliver. Hence, $\hat{\mu}$ should really estimate μ and $\hat{\beta}_2$ should really concern β_2. One way to see whether this is the case amounts to checking whether the expected value of $\hat{\mu}$ is indeed equal to μ. This suggests that if one were able to repeat estimation for samples from a normal distribution with mean μ, one would find an average value of $\hat{\mu}$ which is equal to μ. If this is the case, one says that the estimator is an *unbiased estimator*. For an unbiased estimator it holds that its expected value equals the parameter to be estimated, independent of the number of observations. One can readily see that the $\hat{\mu}$ in (2.11), in the case of normal distribution with mean μ, is an unbiased estimator as

$$E(\hat{\mu}) = \frac{E(y_1) + E(y_2) + \cdots + E(y_n)}{n} = \frac{n\mu}{n} = \mu, \quad (2.16)$$

which illustrates the irrelevance of n.

Although unbiasedness is a useful concept, there seem not to be too many unbiased estimators, simply because it hinges upon a range of assumptions which may not be plausible in practice. Therefore, one is usually satisfied with a *consistent estimator*, which concerns an estimator for which the variance of $\hat{\mu} - \mu$ decreases to zero. The speed at which this closeness gets delivered is called the *rate of convergence*. For the example in (2.13) this rate is $\sqrt{n}$. Consistency is thus related to large samples, and one tends to use phrases like "when my sample grows to *infinity*, the estimator $\hat{\mu}$ would deliver estimates which rapidly approach μ." The notion of an infinite sample, usually denoted as $n \to \infty$, indicates that one examines the *asymptotic behavior* of an estimator.

A second notion is that of *efficiency*. This concept has to do with the fact that in various cases there is not just a single estimator available, but there are many more. In order to compare them, one tends to prefer the estimator which has the smallest variance across estimators for the same parameter. Such an estimator is then called an *efficient estimator*. Hence, efficiency is a relative measure.

The estimator for the mean μ of a normal distribution seems to have a rather obvious expression, but one may wonder how this works for the standard linear regression model in (2.8). Indeed, simply computing averages of observations on y_i and x_i does not work and more subtle methods are needed. As will be discussed in chapter 3, there are various approaches to estimating parameters, but here it suffices to mention just a basic one. This estimation method uses the representation of the regression model, that is,

$$y_i = \beta_1 + \beta_2 x_i + \varepsilon_i, \qquad (2.17)$$

where it can be assumed (although it is not exactly necessary) that

$$\varepsilon_i \sim N(0, \sigma^2). \qquad (2.18)$$

A simple idea would now be that the best match (or *fit*) between y_i and $\hat{\beta}_1 + \hat{\beta}_2 x_i$ would correspond to the case where $\hat{\sigma}^2$ is smallest. Hence, one might look for estimators for β_1

and β_2 for which the residual terms $\hat{\varepsilon}_i$ have the smallest variance $\hat{\sigma}^2$. As an estimator of this variance equals

$$\hat{\sigma}^2 = \frac{(y_1 - \hat{\beta}_1 - \hat{\beta}_2 x_1)^2 + \cdots + (y_n - \hat{\beta}_1 - \hat{\beta}_2 x_n)^2}{n}, \quad (2.19)$$

one may aim to find those values $\hat{\beta}_1$ and $\hat{\beta}_2$ which minimize this sum of squares. In essence, this is the method of *ordinary least squares (OLS)*. At first sight one may think that finding the appropriate estimates amounts to trying out many guesses for $\hat{\beta}_1$ and $\hat{\beta}_2$ and pick those two with the smallest $\hat{\sigma}^2$. However, it turns out that there is what is called the *OLS formula*, and this yields unique and (in some respects) optimal estimators, which are very easy to compute. These estimators are the most reliable among a range of possible estimators.

Some further considerations

In the previous section, it was mentioned that one computes estimators and their standard errors, and other things. One may now wonder how the computations would work. Decades ago, one used to do these computations by hand, but nowadays one uses computers. With these, it takes a fraction of a second to get the OLS estimates for a standard linear regression model. The actual computations are not only fast, in many cases it is also not necessary to write one's own computer programs any more. There are many prefabricated software packages around, like EViews, SPSS,

SAS, Statistica, LimDep, PCGIVE, and others, which only require loading the data and a push on the right button. Well, even if one pushes on the wrong button, present-day packages will tend to start computing something, so it is wise to closely examine what these programs actually do.

A second consideration of practical and theoretical relevance concerns the match between sample and the DGP. This is quite relevant, as in practice one often does not know much about this process. Imagine how a variable like inflation or nondurable consumption can be linked to all kinds of other variables. How can one ever know that sampled data are useful to learn about what is actually going on in the national economy? Usually we cannot, but what we can check is whether there are obvious mistakes. That is, one can see if there are any signs that the model for the sample data needs improvement. This can be done by performing *diagnostic tests* of the model. This sounds a bit like how doctors and plumbers work, who examine whether their ideas about the situation are resistant to further tests, and indeed it comes rather close to it. If diagnostic tests indicate that the model is *misspecified*, one may want to try to improve it. Sometimes one can do that, sometimes one cannot. Two common types of *misspecification* are (1) that one has too many irrelevant variables in one's model, which are called *redundant variables*, or (2) that one has *omitted variables*. The second type is often worse than the first. In the first case, one ends up estimating too many parameters which are effectively zero, and this reduces efficiency of estimators – that is, their associated standard errors become larger than necessary. This is perhaps not so much of a problem, as there are various ways to see which variables are redundant. In some textbooks this is called *model selection*, although perhaps the phrase *variable selection* is better. The second case of omitted variables can be worse as one has overlooked something – that is, the model is lacking components which would have added explanatory value to the model. It sounds like a doctor who misses out a sign of some disease or a plumber who diagnoses a leak at the wrong spot. The econometric model is misspecified and subsequent parameter estimates are often less reliable. This phenomenon is likely to happen in almost all econometric models, in particular in those for complicated economic phenomena. It is hoped, however, that some diagnostic tests will pick it up, or otherwise that the effects of these omitted (and hence unseen) variables are small.

A final issue that should be mentioned here briefly, before this book begins the "guided tour," concerns the implementation of an econometric model. In some cases one is interested in the value of a parameter, for example, a price elasticity. One can use a parameter value to see if some prior thought, like **"Do low values of consumer confidence indicators suggest an upcoming recession?"** gets support from the sample data, or to answer questions like **"what is the price elasticity for second-hand computers?"** In other cases, one can use a model for *forecasting*. Forecasting entails examining or assuming that the model considered for one sample can fruitfully be used for another sample, without having to estimate the parameters for this new sample, too. The implicit assumption is then that these two samples share the same properties. If not, forecasting using the first sample does not make much sense.

A typical example of a situation where forecasting is relevant concerns samples with *time series data*. In this case, one tends to relate an explanatory variable to observations from its own past or to past observations of other variables. The question whether yesterday's NYSE returns correlate (or, explain) today's Amsterdam returns might be answered using the model

$$y_t \sim N(\beta_1 + \beta_2 x_{t-1}, \sigma^2). \tag{2.20}$$

If one believes that past Amsterdam returns have predictive value for its current returns, one may also consider

$$y_t \sim N(\beta_1 + \beta_2 y_{t-1}, \sigma^2), \tag{2.21}$$

which is a *time series model*. From (2.21) it follows that, once one has estimated the parameters with sample data up till T, a forecast for y_{T+1} is $\hat{\beta}_1 + \hat{\beta}_2 y_T$.

To summarize

This chapter has contained a discussion of a few basic concepts in econometrics, which should provide us with an ability to follow most of the discussion in chapters 3 and 4. It should be remembered that for a thorough understanding of these matters, and also for a much better treatment including all details, one should really go ahead and dig into one of the many econometrics textbooks around. So far, I have only discussed some basic tools, and I did not mention how one arrives at certain results and also how one can prove various statements. Also, some additional things – well, in fact a lot more – can be said about all the notions introduced above, but to be able to understand the material in chapters 3 and 4, this will basically do.

In chapter 3, I will outline what interesting practical issues econometricians meet when they aim to answer practically relevant questions. In my experience, not all textbooks are equally informative about these issues, and thereby they can create a gap between theory and practice. In chapter 4, I will show what applied econometrics can look like.

This brings me to a final point, and that concerns the question: "what do academic econometricians effectively do, besides teaching?" Indeed, many economics departments have one or more academics who specialize in econometrics. Besides teaching and administration, these academics most likely spend their time in trying to develop new econometric models (when they face new practical problems that require such new models), developing new estimation methods (either for existing models, or of course for the new ones), and developing new or better diagnostic tests. When academics believe they have developed something relevant, they write it up in a paper and try to present their work at a conference, say, of the Econometric Society, and to have it published in an international refereed journal. Examples of such journals are *Econometrica,* the *Journal of Econometrics,* the *Journal of Applied Econometrics,* and the *Journal of Business and Economic Statistics*. At present, the academic econometric community is a rather active community with among them quite a few Nobel laureates. There are many conferences at which econometricians exchange ideas and new developments, either theoretically or empirically.

CHAPTER THREE

Econometrics, a guided tour

This chapter serves as a review of several of the issues that get raised when one wants to use an econometric model to answer a practical question. The first section of this chapter outlines why I focus on practical problems and not so much on economic theories. The next five sections deal with the five main issues that econometricians have to think about in practice. First one needs to identify and formulate the practical question. Then one has to collect the relevant data that one can consider for answering the question. Next, one combines these two first steps and in many cases a potentially useful econometric model can be chosen. When these matters are all dealt with, the empirical analysis of the model can start. This involves parameter estimation, diagnosing model adequacy, and modification of the model if it is not adequate in some sense. Finally, one tries to implement the model to answer the question.

Practical questions

A long time ago, an econometrician was viewed as an assistant to the economic theorist. The theorist came up with a theory and the econometrician was supposed to collect the relevant data and to show that the theorist was right. Of course, things could go wrong, but that was mainly a matter of concern for the econometrician. In some cases this is still a source of econometric activity, but in my perception this is a rather unfruitful strategy. The difference in the abstraction level of a theory and the practical level of an econometric model is enormous. One can hardly persist in believing that an econometric model amounts to an accurate representation of the theory, and hence can be used to say something about the validity of the theory. Indeed, so many model assumptions have to be made along the way, that any of these can establish eventual rejection or confirmation of a theory. In plain English, there is not much that econometricians can do for theorists (see Summers, 1991, for a rather convincing essay with the same conclusion). Additionally, there is also usually no need to test an economic theory. Economics is not a discipline like physics. Also, there is not a single way to measure a phenomenon. For example, there are lots of possible definitions of unemployment, and their properties can all be different. In sum, I would not recommend using econometric methods to (in-)validate economic theories, as there are always ways out. Also, as Summers argues, the added value of the econometric results is only marginal. He says that key contributions to macroeconomic thinking are not made by econometricians, and frankly, I think he is quite right. So instead of answering a question like "can you prove that my theory is right?" econometricians should rather focus on down-to-earth practical questions, which, when properly answered, can provide interesting insights into the economic issue at stake. Fellow "metricians" do that too. Psychometricians can tell us a lot about individual human behavior, sociometricians tell us about empirical group behavior, cliometricians use advanced methods to interpret historical developments, and biometricians show us how to interpret biological developments. So, would econometricians not be able to say something more about the economy than just a validation of a theory? I believe they would, and in my view, econometricians should aim to summarize relevant economic data in the best possible model for a particular question. The answer to such a question can then be useful to a theorist if s/he is open to it, but also to forecasters, politicians, and managers. Hence, there is no need to limit the scope. In fact, one could even say that econometricians can also discover new statistical regularities in economic data, which in turn might be of interest to theorists to seek for an explanation.

This view does have consequences for teaching and understanding econometrics. First, it is usually assumed that somehow the model is given to the econometrician, as would be true for theory-testers. Also, one has a strong belief in the model. The inconvenient suggestion that the econometric model is not immediately obvious to the econometrician may also explain why people find econometric analysis in practice so difficult. As mentioned earlier, a common question I get from my workshop students is "how do I start?" And indeed, there are different models for different purposes.

An additional assumption often made, which is also something one rarely encounters in practice, is that the relevant data are all available and properly measured. This is not always true, and to me it seems therefore important to discuss data collection in more detail. This should be done prior to choosing the model, especially as the type of data often already partially suggests the shape of the subsequent model.

Therefore, I would like to pay specific attention to these topics, in reverse order. First, I would like to focus on a few questions, and in particular on their degree of precision. Next, I treat data collection, and after that I discuss how these two can come together into an econometric model.

Problem formulation

The main issue to be put forward in this section is that anyone who wants to use an econometric model to answer a question should bear in mind that the question must be very precisely stated. If not, then about everything goes, and the resulting empirical results are not trustworthy, at least not in relation to the question. An important consequence of such precision is that subsequent decisions depend on it. For example, when the aim is to set up a model for twenty years' ahead forecasting, it is conceivable that such a model will differ from a model that can answer what is going on in the first few seconds of a trading day on the stock market.

To discuss precision, let me first briefly consider the example which is also used in Granger (1999, pp. 42–48), and then proceed with another example. Hall (1978) argues that the Life-Cycle Permanent Income Hypothesis entails that non-durable consumption y_t can be described by a random walk model, that is,

$$y_t = \beta_1 + \beta_2 y_{t-1} + \varepsilon_t, \qquad (3.1)$$

with $\beta_2 = 1$. Leaving aside the assumptions that led to this theory, and whether they are valid or not, the focus here is on (3.1). At first sight one would think that this is a rather precise statement, but unfortunately it is not for two reasons. The first is that there is no discussion of the observation frequency for which this model should hold. Indeed, as Granger (1999) also indicates, if this model held for monthly data, it by definition would not hold for quarterly data, as temporal aggregation entails that the model requires additional explanatory variables. Additionally, the key aspect of the theory is that $\beta_2 = 1$, which in time series jargon is defined as saying that y_t has a *unit root*. As the last twenty years of theoretical and empirical econometric research have shown, statistically testing whether $\beta_2 = 1$ is notoriously difficult (and, some say, even impossible). In sum, the theory may be nice, but data would not be indicative enough that this theory could be wrong. It the theory had predicted that non-durable consumption could be described by (3.1) in which β_2 would cover an interval which includes 1, one would have had a better chance.

Another frequently encountered hypothesis, predominantly of interest in finance, is the efficient market hypothesis. This hypothesis goes back to Samuelson (1965) who proves that the best forecast for the value of the next stock price P_{t+1} equals the current price. Campbell, Lo and MacKinlay (1997) provide an interesting review of an array of methods to examine whether this theory holds. One of these is to see whether the natural log transformed price series can be described by

$$\log P_t = \log P_{t-1} + \varepsilon_t, \qquad (3.2)$$

where ε_t is assumed to have mean zero and variance σ^2. Sometimes it is even assumed that ε_t is normally distributed. This hypothesis makes sense, as if all traders knew the same, then arbitrage opportunities would not exist or would at least disappear very quickly. The key issue, however, is whether traders have the same information and if they all interpret it in the same way. Also, if (3.2) were true, can stock market crashes happen? Hence, again it seems that though (3.2) looks like a rather precise statement, to really be able to be a bit more conclusive on whether people trade efficiently on average, it seems that one should sit next to traders and to ask them why they do what they do. And does (3.2) hold for every minute or second of a trading day, and does it hold for all stocks or only for aggregates?

There are many more illustrative examples we could give, but the above two should suffice to indicate that, at least to me, it seems that testing an economic theory is perhaps not a good starting point for the specification of an econometric model. Indeed, when the data reject the theory, the theorist will say that the econometrician must have done something wrong, and when there is no rejection, the theorist is happy, but fellow econometricians may come along to say that one used an inappropriate method. This, by the way, is perhaps one of the main reasons that econometricians still (in 2002) do not know what is the best method to test for the so-called *random walk hypothesis*, that is, $\beta_2 = 1$ in (3.1). Second, the above examples show that the specification of an econometric model also needs input from the properties of the data relevant to the problem at hand.

One may now wonder how one should come up with more precise guidelines for the construction of an econometric model. These guidelines should follow from rather precise questions. Examples of a few of these questions appear in chapter 4, but here I discuss a few. Going back to the examples above, one way to get insights in whether a theory makes sense is not to ask whether a random walk model fits the data, but to ask **"how can I beat the random walk?"** which is effectively done in various empirical studies. Additionally, in order to give a model a fair chance, by refining this question, one may think of asking **"how** can I beat the random walk in out-of-sample forecast-ing?" As the random walk model is rather powerful when it comes to one-step-ahead forecasting, and this holds almost uniformly across economic and other disciplines, an even more precise statement is "can I construct an economet-ric model that beats the random walk in forecasting many steps ahead?" Indeed, if one removes from the ran-dom walk model even for faraway horizons, the econometric model is not of much value, as the ten-step-ahead forecast from (3.1) is simply $\log P_{T+10} = \log P_T$.

Aggregation over time or individuals matters, too. If one believes that total nondurable consumption follows a ran-dom walk, how should all of its components behave? So, it may pay off just to zoom in on one of the components and to examine its behavior. For example, a question can be "are mid-sized cars equally expensive in Japan and in the USA, after correction for the exchange rate between these two countries?" Leaving aside whether this is in-teresting or not, it seems a better question than "does the purchasing power parity hypothesis hold for Japan and the USA?" Note that the question has its origins in economic theoretical considerations. Economic theory often says something about the *long run*. Hence by definition one is barely able to verify the resulting statements. Therefore, a focus on short-run statements might be much more fruitful. For example, a question that incorporates this is "if there is some potential of predicting the next period stock return of a company, for how many steps ahead can

I use this information?" and another is **"how long do deviations from a long-run price equilibrium in Japan and the USA last?"**

So far, I have discussed examples which somehow match with an economic theory, as this seems to correspond with a common notion in econometrics. Of course, this does not have to be the case, and many practical questions faced by an econometrician do not originate from economic theories. One may simply be interested in the correlation across variables, while acknowledging the possibility that other variables of less interest also have an effect. For example, **"what is the price elasticity of coffee in this supermarket, and does it differ across brands?"** or **"did the recent employment program lead to more new jobs than there would have been without it?"** or **"do so-called psychological barriers, like 10,000 points, have an effect on stock market volatility?"** One may also be interested in just forecasting various steps ahead. So, a relevant question can be **"can I get an accurate forecast for next month's new car sales?"** or **"do London FTSE daily stock returns have predictive content for the Nikkei returns?"** or **"what is the time lag between explosive growth in hardware sales and the take-off in software sales, and can this be used for out-of-sample forecasting of software sales?"**

Another use of econometric models amounts to, in fact, historical analysis. Indeed, there have been several post-war macroeconomic recessions, and one may wonder whether there were any indicators which could have predicted a recession. If so, one might use the same indicators to suggest the likelihood of future recessions. Hence, relevant questions can be **"did wage rigidity lead to excessive unemployment prior to recessions?"** or **"do monthly observed consumer sentiment indicators have predictive value for retail sales?** or **"is a higher demand for money a sign of an upcoming recession?"** Note that one still needs to define what a "recession" is, but there are consensus definitions around. For other examples above, the same remarks can be made on measurement, and therefore I turn to this topic in the next section.

In sum, I argue that simply following many of the available economic theories does not lead to precise enough statements which can fruitfully be translated into a useful econometric model. Of course, if there are any theoretical arguments around, it is unwise to dismiss them, but otherwise one needs to introduce more precision. When doing so, it is good to bear in mind that theories usually deal with aggregate measures, like "inflation," "unemployment," or "sales," while the econometrician can make a selection among lots of inflation series, unemployment in various categories and in various countries, and among sales across lots of stores, products, brands, and time. Hence, before one formulates a practical question which may lead to an econometric model, one first needs to have a look at the available data.

Data collection

The issue of data collection is rarely addressed in econometric textbooks, but also in applied econometric work there is rarely a discussion on why and how one did collect the data that were used in the applied study. This may seem a bit odd, as it is well understood that the final conclusions in all studies crucially depend on the nature and quality of the data selected. In this section I say a few words on this matter by first discussing some data sources, and then mentioning something about data transformations and frequently encountered problems with empirical data.

Data sources

Before one starts collecting data, it is important to define what one means by certain variables in the practical question. In various economic disciplines it can be fairly clear how one should collect data. In finance, for example, there is no debate as to what today's closing rate of the Amsterdam Stock Exchange index is. However, in the same area one has to deal with concepts as "emerging markets" or "AAA-rated firms," and these are all just defined from the outset. In marketing it is pretty obvious what dollar sales are, but how should one measure the price? Is the relevant price the price with (the shelf price) or without price promotions? At a more aggregated level, these issues become even more pronounced. What exactly is "industrial production" or "durable consumption?" And, what is "inflation?" Does inflation measure all products, including high-tech computers, and, if so, how many of these are included in the basket, which also contains eggs, toilet paper, and cars? Too many questions, possibly, but it does give a clear suggestion that questions like **"is the current high inflation a sign of upcoming increases in wages?"** or **"are emerging financial markets less stable than developed markets?"** are far from trivial to answer.

There are various sources for economic data that can be considered for an econometric model. Roughly speaking, there are three main types of data. A first type is what is called *cross-section data*. Usually this concerns observations on n individuals, where one should read "individuals" in a broad sense, as it can also concern other entities like firms and countries. Sample sizes can be like 100 or 1,000, but larger than 10,000 is quite rare. Sometimes one can collect information by actual measurement using annual reports of firms or actual tax statements of individuals. In other cases, one has to collect the data using a survey or by conducting an experiment. It should also be stressed that actual measurements are usually what are called *revealed preference data (RP)*, and hence these data concern what actually happened. In some cases, one cannot get such RP data – as, for example, the sales of a new product that are not yet available. In that case one can resort to collecting *stated preference data (SP)*. One should then hope that these SP data have predictive value for the eventually revealed preferences, although in some situations one may use these two data sources in combination (see Louviere, Hensher and Swait, 2000 and Verhoef, Franses and Hoekstra, 2001 for recent accounts).

A second source of economic data concerns *repeated cross-sections*, meaning that one observes the behavior of individuals over time. When these are the same individuals, the resulting data are called *panel data*. Examples of panel data are household panels who document all purchases in each week, or panels of countries for which certain economic characteristics are observed, or panels of firms for which financial variables have been measured over a number of years. One reason why one might consider panel data is that there may be some common properties across the individuals over time, such that there is no need to consider n independent regression models. For example, suppose one has data on n individuals for T time periods, then one may consider extending the standard linear regression model as

$$y_{i,t} = \beta_{i,1} + \beta_{i,2} x_{i,t} + \varepsilon_{i,t}, \qquad (3.3)$$

where the index (i, t) concerns an observation for individual i at time t. One may now assume that $\beta_{i,1} = \beta_1$ and $\beta_{i,2} = \beta_2$, but one can also consider for example that

$$\beta_{i,2} \sim N(\beta_2, \sigma_\beta^2). \qquad (3.4)$$

One then says that, averaged over individuals and time, the effect of the explanatory variable is β_2, but that there are possible deviations from this effect across the individuals. Panel data are not as widely available as cross-section data.

Usually, one has to collect them oneself, and this can amount to a lot of work.

A third source of data can be viewed as a *condensed panel data set*, where either the number of individuals is equal to 1 or where the data have been averaged over the *n* individuals resulting in a single variable. Examples are daily stock returns for Royal Dutch Petroleum and returns on the Amsterdam Stock Exchange, respectively. Note that time series data in turn can also be aggregated over time – that is, stock market data can be available for each second, one minute, five minutes, days, months, and years. Macroeconomic data are usually available on a monthly basis, while sales and market shares are typically obtained at a weekly frequency. Time series data have become quite popular for analysis since 1980. Perhaps this is mainly owing to the fact that they can be obtained more easily than panels and cross-sections. Statistical agencies publish macroeconomic indicators, various companies provide financial data, and some market research firms are willing to give one a look at their data sources (although usually with a time lag of a couple of years).

The natural question is of course **"which data source should I use?"** Assuming that the observations are reliable, the common answer would be "the more, the better." Indeed, if one aims at answering **"does inflation lead to fewer retail sales?"** one can opt for analyzing quarterly observed macroeconomic data. However, if one can also analyze a panel of 4,000 households who document their purchases and the associated prices during a few years, one might get more precise answers. In fact, in general, the more data one has, the more precise one can be. Also, the nature of the question can be adjusted. If those 4,000 households live spread over the country and do shopping in a variety of retail stores, one might believe that their joint behavior reflects total retail sales. However, if one measures only clothing and shoe sales, then the information from the panel is limited, at least for the particular question on average inflation. At the other end, if there are almost no data, one should be more modest in the question. An assignment to predict sales for the next ten years while only three years of annual data are available is possible only if one copies the results for other, say, countries.

More data, however, usually also implies more model, in the sense that the econometric model becomes more complicated and the corresponding parameter estimators might become more involved. Indeed, one can quickly appreciate that the estimator for β_2 in (3.4) is more involved than that for the β_2 in the standard regression model. Hence, other data and other models may lead to other estimators. Also, for cross-sectional data it may be more easy to assume that the data constitute a random sample. For time series observations this is a little more difficult as tomorrow's observation on inflation will on average depend heavily on today's inflation. Usually, this is not so much of a problem, although it can happen that if one forgets about this time-dependency of time series observations, one can get spurious results. For example, suppose a sales variable S_t in dollars can be described by a so-called *first order autoregressive model*, that is,

$$S_t = \rho_1 + \rho_2 S_{t-1} + \varepsilon_t, \tag{3.5}$$

and that the firm takes for advertising A_t the budgeting rule that

$$A_t = \delta_1 + \delta_2 S_{t-1} + v_t, \tag{3.6}$$

where v_t measures some erratic deviations from this budgeting rule. Hence, current advertising is a fraction of previous sales. One can now easily find an effect of advertising on sales from the regression model

$$S_t = \tau_1 + \tau_2 A_t + \zeta_t, \tag{3.7}$$

that is, a significant value of $\hat{\tau}_2$, while in reality there is no direct effect of advertising on sales. This effect immediately disappears when one also includes S_{t-1} in (3.7), thereby indicating that the past of the sales variable should be included in order to prevent one drawing inappropriate conclusions.

Finally, an often-heard question is **"how many data should I collect?"** Interestingly, this question is hard and often not possible to answer. The main reason is that one rarely knows all the properties of the sample observations. If one knew this, then one could say something about the sample size. For example, when tossing a coin one knows the population, and one can ask **"how many coins do I need to analyze such that I can say with 99.9 per cent confidence that the coins in the population are**

all proper coins?" However, if the DGP entails the relations between one dependent variable and many explanatory variables, one most likely has no clue. What is certain, though, is that if one can collect disaggregated data, these are to be preferred for the simple reason that one can always aggregate disaggregated data but usually not the other way around. Moreover, one should bear in mind that the entire analysis assumes that the data originate from one and the same DGP. When one aims to forecast next month's total inflation (all items), it may be doubtful whether pre-war data are useful for this exercise. Indeed, one may think that these data are to be associated with another era, and also that they must have concerned many different goods than the ones included nowadays.

Data transformations

It is quite common that econometricians or other individuals transform the observed data prior to analysis. Such transformations can concern aggregation over individuals or over time, but other linear and nonlinear transformations are also possible. Whatever transformation is used, it is important to be aware of the fact that these transformations can have an effect on the interpretation of the model and its parameters and it can have an effect on estimators, as they might need correction.

A common transformation is *aggregation*. Examples of aggregated variables, where aggregation concerns individual variables, are the Standard and Poor's 500 stock index

(S&P500), total industrial production, total retail sales in all stores of a certain chain, and inflation. It is important to understand that the properties of the underlying individual series get reflected in the aggregated variable. In many cases this is not something to become very nervous about, but it may be useful for further analysis. If one analyzes volatility in S&P500 returns, it can be of interest to assign the source of this volatility to just one or two of its components. A possibly relevant question is then **"is excess volatility in the SP500 due to excess volatility in oil-based assets?"** Furthermore, examples of variables which are the result of temporal aggregation are annual retail sales, monthly stock returns, and quarterly industrial production, as these variables are typically measured at a higher frequency.

The interesting aspect of aggregation is that there are no rules whatsoever to decide on the *optimal level* of aggregation, if such a concept did exist. Hence, it can sometimes be wise to analyze the components and then join the results in order to examine the aggregate, but sometimes it is not. For example, in order to forecast all-items inflation, would it be sensible to forecast all component inflation series and then aggregate the forecasts, or is it better to consider the aggregate right away? Well, this all depends on the properties of these series. For example, if the component series suffer from structural breaks, but these happen at the same time, using the last series seems most convenient. The same holds true for temporal aggregation. Suppose one has to answer **"what are the best forecasts for next year's new**

computer sales?" one can make a choice between modeling the annual data and generating forecasts or modeling the monthly data (assuming these are available), generating twelve forecasts and then aggregating these. As far as I know, there is no firm rule that says that one is better than the other. However, if one does have a choice, it seems sensible to consider the data which are most easily summarized in a model.

Where one does not have enough data, one may try to create more by *interpolation*. Suppose there are only annual data available and one needs to say something about the quarterly data, one can sometimes create these data by interpolation. Such interpolation can, for example, be based on the intra-year patterns of other variables. In fact, it so happens that, prior to the 1970s, some macroeconomic variables for some countries were constructed along these lines. This means that when one is constructing an econometric model for early data, one might end up modeling the very method that was used to create the data. In other words, it seems useful to check with the data provider how the data were collected.

Another way of creating more time series data amounts to generating overlapping data. Suppose one has only five years' of quarterly data, then one can also create annual data by each time considering four consecutive quarters. As such, one can create fourteen observations on annual data, where of course these observations have become temporally dependent. Owing to this, one needs to modify certain estimators. Take for example the basic case where there is a sample of $T + q - 1$ observations on a variable x_t, with q indicating the degree of overlap, where it is known that

$$x_t \sim N(0, \sigma^2). \tag{3.8}$$

Next, suppose one considers the q-period overlapping variable y_t which is constructed as

$$y_1 = x_1 + x_2 + \cdots + x_q, \tag{3.9}$$

$$y_2 = x_2 + x_3 + \cdots + x_{q+1}, \ldots, \tag{3.10}$$

$$y_T = x_T + x_{T+1} + \cdots + x_{T+q-1}. \tag{3.11}$$

Given (3.8), the variance of y_t is $q\sigma^2$. In Bod *et al.* (2002) it is derived that an unbiased estimator for this variance is equal to

$$\hat{\sigma}^2 = \frac{(y_1 - \hat{\mu})^2 + (y_2 - \hat{\mu})^2 + \cdots + (y_T - \hat{\mu})^2}{T - q + \frac{1}{3}\frac{q^2-1}{T}}, \tag{3.12}$$

where $\hat{\mu}$ is the sample mean of y_t. Campbell, Lo and MacKinlay (1997) consider another factor than

$$T - q + \frac{1}{3}\frac{q^2 - 1}{T},$$

but this does not give an unbiased estimator. The main purpose of this exercise is to show that seemingly simple transformations of data can lead to rather complicated expressions of useful estimators. Notice that one can find out about these expressions only if one knows how the data got constructed. If one does not, which in this case means that the value of q would be unknown, then there is not much an econometrician can do.

The familiar situation where econometricians may have to handle data that someone else has created, without telling exactly how, emerges when one has to analyze seasonally adjusted data (where adjustment was done using what is called the Census X-12 technique). Such data usually amount to filtered original data, where the exact filter can be unknown. In other words, the econometrician has to handle estimated data, being unaware of the associated confidence bounds in most cases. To my knowledge, seasonal adjustment happens only in macroeconomics, also perhaps owing to the fact that statements like "the Dow Jones went up today, but, as it is Monday, it really went down" would be widely considered as hilarious. Nowadays one tends also to make available the original data, and hence one can use these to make econometric models. This is an important issue in macroeconometric modeling as Census X-12 seasonally adjusted data are effectively also not meant to get summarized by models. First of all, owing to the seasonal adjustment treatment the data tend to get properties they did not have before, and also important information gets lost. Second, one cannot analyze the estimated residuals in the corresponding models and try to assign an interpretation to these in terms of innovations, as the relevant information is filtered out too. Finally, out-of-sample forecasts of seasonally adjusted data are hard to evaluate as the adjusted data simply do not get observed. In sum, when one is able to use the raw data for econometric models, it is always better to do so (see also Franses, 2001).

Finally, there are also a few reasonably harmless data transformations, and they usually amount to taking squares or natural logarithms of the data. For example in the model

$$\log y_i = \beta_1 + \beta_2 \log x_i + \varepsilon_i, \qquad (3.13)$$

the parameter β_2 is a constant elasticity, while in the original regression model without logs the elasticity would be $\beta_2 \frac{x_i}{y_i}$. Even though econometricians tend to routinely apply the log transformation, it is good to bear in mind what it does to the model. Finally, in some cases one may want to forecast levels, like the amount of individuals who are unemployed, as well as growth rates, which can be approximated by $\log x_t - \log x_{t-1}$. The model for y_t can also be used for getting forecasts for these growth rates, but there is no particular reason why this should always hold.

Data problems

A topic that is even more often overlooked in econometrics textbooks, and hence for which many students are often totally unprepared when they make their first steps into practice, concerns data problems. Obviously, it is not a pleasant topic, but it is something that simply cannot be ignored. There are various types of data problems, but the most frequently encountered ones are *missing data* and the possibility that the collected data are *not random*. The combination of the two is the worst, and this can occur quite frequently when conducting surveys among individuals.

Missing data can concern missing observations on relevant variables, but it may also concern having no observations on relevant variables. The last situation is usually known as the *omitted variables* problem. Unfortunately it is difficult to avoid suffering from omitted variables, and usually it is hoped that these variables are either not too important or that they are somehow unrelated to the others.

Sometimes there are ways of getting around omitted variables. For example, in surveys where one asks individuals to agree or disagree with statements and where one observes some individual-specific characteristics, it is quite likely that these characteristics cannot fully explain people's attitudes and opinions. This means that the standard regression model cannot fully describe the relation between the y_i variable and the x_i variables. One way out of this is to translate this so-called *unobserved heterogeneity* into varying parameters. This approach is pretty popular in marketing research.

This first type of missing data concerns a lack of data for one or more of the potentially useful variables. An obvious example is annual time series data for which the intermediate quarterly data are not available. Another frequently occurring example for cross-section data is that surveyed individuals do not answer all questions. If this happens at random – for example, because one has lost pages of the questionnaires for a few individuals – then one may think of replacing the missing data by average values, obtained from the completed surveys. This method of *imputation* is often applied, and if one has to work with such a data set it is always important to ask the data provider what s/he actually did. Sometimes, imputation is a little more complicated, as one then replaces the missing observation by some forecast from a model for the other data or one asks the question in a more clever way. The latter means that one might get answers to questions people feel uncomfortable with in answering, like in the USA "do you or did you ever smoke marihuana?" or in the Netherlands "what is your monthly income?" Finally, it is also possible that you simply sent the questionnaires to the wrong individuals. For example, if one sent out a questionnaire to managers asking them **"do you use advanced models for your everyday decisions?"** they would obviously say "no," simply because it is not their job to use these models.

The problem with many missing data, however, is that they rarely are missing at random. In fact, it seems always wise to ask the question: why are some data missing? When one is following households and their purchase behavior over time, then some households may decide to quit. If this decision is based on the fact that they move to another country, there should not be much of a problem, but if this decision is based on the fact that they became bored with becoming so price-aware, then the very reason to observe these households in the first place (which is to examine price-sensitivity) causes people to quit. This is what is called *nonrandom attrition*, and one has to take account of it when computing price elasticities. The opposite of attrition is that only a few people are in the sample and that being a member of that group is established by the very topic of interest. For example, one can examine why and how much individuals donate to charity only if they received an invitation letter to do so. That is, those who do not receive a direct mailing do not donate. Interestingly, according to most currently available so-called "targeting rules," those who receive a letter have often donated frequently in the past (see also chapter 4 below).

A nonrandom sample usually introduces a *sample selection bias*. Although the phrase sample selection sounds like "selecting a sample for analysis," which sounds not harmful, in reality it is. If one does not account for the nonrandomness of the sample, many empirical outcomes will be flawed. For example, take a school reunion and suppose one is interested in measuring the average salary of the school's alumni. Anyone who feels unsuccessful in life might not be there, which implies that one might easily overrate the quality of the school. This example already suggests that the estimator for the average salary is biased.

Roughly speaking, there are two ways out in case of sample selection effects. The first is to also keep on collecting data for the group of individuals who are underrepresented. This might be very costly or sometimes impossible, and therefore the second option, which is to adapt the estimator, is most commonly considered. There is an abundance of correcting estimators, and this area is certainly not recommended as a first foray into econometrics. The main idea is that one somehow incorporates the selection process into the model. Hence, the model can consist of two components, one which describes how the data were collected, and one the model of interest.

Finally, another data problem occurs when some observations have an unduly large effect on inference. These observations may be labeled as *influential observations*. Such observations can be owing to keying errors, and hence one says that they are not really of interest to the econometrician, or they may just simply be large owing to some combination of factors. A good example is the stock market crash in 1987, which on Monday September 19 amounted to a negative Dow Jones return of 22.8 per cent. This can hardly be viewed as a keying error, but the question is to what extent this value is excessive, in the sense that no model could have predicted such a large and negative return. In other words, might it be that part of the observation has nothing to do with the underlying DGP? Hence, one may wonder whether this observation could somehow be discounted when estimating parameters. If one wants to do so, one has to rely on *robust estimation methods*. Basically, robust estimation can amount to finding the parameters which minimize

$$\hat{\sigma}^2 = \frac{w_1(y_1 - \hat{\beta}_1 - \hat{\beta}_2 x_1)^2 + \cdots + w_n(y_n - \hat{\beta}_1 - \hat{\beta}_2 x_n)^2}{n},$$

$$(3.14)$$

where the weights w_i are to be assigned by the researcher. There are ways to let the data tell you which observations get which weights. Note that this approach can also be used to handle structural breaks – that is, when some parts of the data look different from others.

To conclude, when analyzing data one should always wonder **"where do the data come from?"** and **"how were they collected?"** and also **"can it possibly be that not all relevant data are available, and hence that the sample is perhaps not random?"** If one trusts there are no problems, one can proceed with the search for a proper model. Otherwise, one first needs to collect more or better data, or adapt the estimators to this situation.

Choice of an econometric model

This and the next section deal with the aspects which are treated in many textbooks. I will be rather brief on these issues, as I believe that if one has clear ideas about the practical question – that is, one has been able to precisely formulate it – and that one is confident that the relevant data are available and are properly measured, the subsequent steps are sometimes not that complicated. Of course, one needs experience and skill for this. I do not mean to say that it is all easy – that is, that parameter estimation is easy, that variable selection is easy, that using diagnostic measures is easy. However, it is my belief that once one has precise ideas of how to answer the question and one has the data, two very important steps have been made. In sum, it is from now on assumed that one knows what y_i or y_t is and one knows the explanatory variables, and that one has observations on all these variables.

Our attention is now confined to the selection of a useful and relevant econometric model. Note that I do not mean *variable selection* here, as this amounts to looking for the best x_is (among other candidates) to explain y_i. The focus is on selecting a model like

$$y_i \sim N(\beta_1 + \beta_2 x_i, \sigma^2). \tag{3.15}$$

Obviously, the normal distribution is not the only distribution around, and indeed there are many other distributions. Some knowledge of these can come in handy now, as sometimes the y_i can be hardly called a normal variable, not even conditional on explanatory variables. For example, there are applications where y_i can take only the values 1 and 0, where 1 denotes "yes, this individual donated to charity" and 0 means "no, s/he did not donate." A simple idea to see how one can handle such a *binary dependent variable* is to replace the normal distribution in (3.15) by the Bernoulli distribution (see also Franses and Paap, 2001, for similar treatments of various other types of variables which typically occur in marketing research). In general, one can write for such a binary variable

$$y_i \sim B(\pi), \tag{3.16}$$

where π is the unknown parameter. When tossing a coin, one knows that π in the population is 0.5. As in the linear regression model, one can now replace π by an expression which reflects that it is conditional on an explanatory variable. As π is a probability and hence is bounded between 0 and 1, one choice could be to replace π by $F(\frac{\beta_1+\beta_2 x_i}{\sigma})$, where $F(.)$ is a function which gives values between 0 and 1. If $F(.)$ is the cumulative density function (cdf) of the standard normal distribution, this model is the *probit model*. Note by the way that this model seeks to relate an explanatory variable x_i with the probability that y_i is 1 or 0 and not with the exact value of y_i.

In sum, the choice for the proper econometric model heavily depends on the properties of y_i. The properties of the explanatory variables are often of less relevance, and hence the focus is not so much on the x_i variables here. As some econometric models are not linear in the parameters, as also is the probit model above, it can be useful to examine the meaning of the parameters and the genuine effect of changes in x_i. A simple tool for this is to examine the elasticities of x_i on y_i.

Once one has decided on the type of model, one sometimes needs to make a further choice between various competitors by examining what the models actually can do and what they mean. This is particularly relevant when analyzing time series data, as there are models that can generate data with the very same features. To provide an example, consider the model

$$y_t = \delta + y_{t-1} + \varepsilon_t, \tag{3.17}$$

and compare it with

$$y_t = \mu + \delta t + \varepsilon_t, \qquad (3.18)$$

where $t = 1, 2, \ldots, T$, and where ε_t is an unpredictable zero-mean variable with variance σ^2. It is easy to understand that (3.18) can describe a variable which displays a trending pattern, simply owing to the fact that the model contains the trend variable t. However, the model in (3.17) can also describe a variable with a trend. This can be understood from the fact that at any time t, the observation equals the previous one plus some value δ, on average. Indeed, when the δ in the two equations is the same, and the variance of ε_t is reasonably small, one has serious trouble making a distinction between the two by just looking at their graphs. However, the two models are fundamentally different for various reasons, one of which can be understood from looking at their forecasts. Suppose one needs to forecast two steps ahead, which seems quite reasonable for a trending variable, then for the model in (3.17) the observation at $T + 2$ is

$$y_{T+2} = 2\delta + y_T + \varepsilon_{T+2} + \varepsilon_{T+1}. \qquad (3.19)$$

As the best forecasts for the innovations are 0, the effective forecast boils down to $2\delta + y_t$, which gives a squared forecast error of $2\sigma^2$, as one misses out ε_{T+2} and ε_{T+1}, which are assumed to be independent. When one considers the model in (3.18), the observation at $T + 2$ is

$$y_{T+2} = \mu + \delta(T + 2) + \varepsilon_{T+2}, \qquad (3.20)$$

and the squared forecast error here is just σ^2. So, even though both models can describe a trending variable with the same trend, the first model yields more uncertainty about its forecasts than the second. The distinction between the two models in practice is rather difficult. It has been bothering academic econometricians now for the last two decades, under the heading of *"testing for unit roots."*

In sum, in many cases the way the dependent variable has been observed dictates the ultimate shape of the econometric model. In various other cases, one should be aware of the possibility that different – or, at least, different-looking – models can be used for the same purposes. If they do, one may need to make a further selection between these models. A possible complexity is then that the models may not be *nested*. This means that one model does not pop up from the other when one or more parameters are set equal to zero. In fact, the two models in (3.17) and (3.18) are not nested, although one can combine the explanatory variables into a single model.

Empirical analysis

There are a lot of issues still to consider once one has a clear sight of the practical question, the data and the model. The first issue is that one needs to estimate the *unknown parameters*. There are many ways of doing that, and various empirical considerations can also point towards alternatives. Next, one needs to diagnose whether the model is in some sense *good or not.* This is rather important as a serious mismatch between the model and the data implies that all conclusions are flawed. Finally, one can try to *modify the model* if this turns out to be necessary.

Estimation of parameters

In chapter 2 one could already see that it is possible to estimate unknown parameters, and, with these and their associated standard errors, to say something about their relevance. Indeed, one does not really know whether price promotions lead to more sales, and hence data and a model can indicate if this is perhaps the case, with some de-gree of confidence. It is important to stress here again that the phrase "estimate" should be taken rather seriously, as one can never be sure with practical data. The only thing we are sure of is a statement like "with 100 per cent confidence I forecast that tomorrow's weather can be like anything," but those statements would not generate great confidence in one's forecasting abilities. Econometricians therefore tend to say that **"with 95 per cent confidence it is believed that price promotions lead to more sales,"** which is the same statement as **"the effect of price promotions on sales is not zero at the 5 per cent significance level."**

As estimation entails saying something about what is un-known, one can imagine that there are more ways to esti-mate parameters than the OLS method already discussed. In fact, finding out new ways of estimating parameters for old and new models is one of the favorite pastimes of academic econometricians. A nice feature these days is that one can evaluate various methods using computer simulations. Econometricians can sometimes rely on formal proofs that one estimator is more efficient than another, but in other cases one can set up numerical experiments to see which estimator is best. A drawback of these simulation experiments, which are usually called *Monte Carlo simulations*, is that they can be dependent on the simulation design, while mathematical proofs would make differences between assumptions very clear. The omnipresent focus on estimation in textbooks is of course initiated by the fact that without estimated values for unknown parameters, the whole exercise of trying to answer a question stops. Additionally, inappropriate estimators can lead to rather silly results, even for a large sample. Bod *et al.* (2002) show that the consistent but not unbiased estimator of the variance of overlapping returns gives rather poor outcomes even in large samples. Hence, working through the mathematics to get an unbiased estimator, as Bod *et al.* (2002) did, really pays off. In other cases, as Den Haan and Levin (1997) lucidly illustrate, the performance of rival estimators might become noticeably different only when there are so many observations as one in reality rarely has. For practical purposes it is always good to know whether the estimator works.

There are various other methods to estimate parameters than simply using OLS. One type of method still takes on board the idea of least squares, but it allows for data features or model mistakes and takes these into account when estimating the parameters. An example of a specific data feature concerns influential observations. An example of a model mistake concerns the assumption that all ε_i have a common variance while in reality it is σ_i^2. Such methods are simply called *generalized least squares*. Another often-used variant is *nonlinear least squares*, which is usually applied to models which include variables which, as one says, are non-linear in the parameters, such as $\beta_2 x_i^\gamma$.

A common phrase when estimating model parameters is the *degrees of freedom*. This is a rather fascinating concept, which can be viewed as the difference between the number of observations in the sample and the number of unknown parameters that one needs to estimate. Zero degrees of freedom occur when there is not much to say about uncertainty. Going back to the one-variable regression model, if one has only two pairs of observations on y and x, then $\hat{\beta}_1$ and $\hat{\beta}_2$ give a perfect fit. This seems nice, but it is not, as one cannot say anything about the quality of the estimated parameter values. Perhaps this is even more clear when one tosses a coin just once. It is certain that the coin will indicate either heads or tails, but obtaining heads once does not allow us to say anything about the underlying population. Here we see a trade-off between fit and uncertainty which is not that trivial. Having a lot degrees of freedom allows one to make statements with greater confidence, while having no freedom left renders a perfect fit. Again, this last precision is just seemingly useful, as if one had tossed another coin, or taken two other pairs of data on y and x, one could have concluded something completely different. Hence, the rule of thumb for most econometricians is to try and have as many degrees of freedom as possible. This usually means that one tries to arrive at a rather *parsimonious model*, which entails not too many variables, and hence not too many parameters to estimate.

There are at least two approaches to estimation which are rather different from least squares in a more philosophical sense, although it must be stressed that sometimes one would not get very different answers to practical questions. The first is what is called the *Maximum Likelihood (ML)* method. In words, the ML method tries to find those $\hat{\beta}_1$ and $\hat{\beta}_2$ in the standard regression model which imply that the observed values for y_i are the most likely values. This is quite a nice concept as it asks, for example, what is behind the observed retail sales that most likely generated these data. As such, the ML method becomes intermediary between the observations in the sample and the DGP with its unknown properties. For some models, like for example the probit model discussed earlier, the ML method is the most reliable method, while for other models one may want to choose between least squares and ML.

Another frequently applied method is the so-called *Bayesian method*. The Bayesian method abstains from the notion that one might repeat drawing samples from a population. When tossing a coin one can do that, but when analyzing, say, quarterly *per capita* GDP, one cannot. Indeed, there is only one observation on GDP each quarter, and having another look at the data does not give another value. The sample is taken as the starting point and the question asked **"can we learn about the data given that we measure them only once?"** If the model is well specified, and with *prior* thoughts about the parameter values, one can use the sample observations to get what is called a *posterior distribution* of the parameters. Hence, it is not only the distributional assumption that gives a confidence interval, it is the combined effort of the data, the model, and the prior. This implies that Bayesian econometricians have a strong belief in the quality of their model (although there are ways to assign uncertainty to that, too), that they need to be confident about their priors, and that they are also able to communicate the relevance of these priors. Bayesian analysis used to be technically difficult and computationally demanding, but with modern computer power many problems can be solved by using simulation techniques (see Paap, 2002 for an excellent survey).

Now it does so happen that some Bayesian econometricians and some least squares or ML econometricians believe that they have universal truth on their side. Indeed, the two self-proclaimed philosophies do approach econometric analysis from different angles but, to me, there seems to be value in both. Also, for answering practical questions it is merely a matter of taste or convenience than that one can really demonstrate that one approach persistently leads to radically different answers than the other.

Finally, many estimation routines have been encapsulated in commercial statistical software packages. The basic activity of these packages is to estimate parameters, as the researcher has to import the data, define the model, and has to interpret the results. So, all programs just do the estimation. By the way, current packages are quite smart, which means they do not crash when something goes wrong (as they did when I was a student and made a keying error). The user gets information that s/he is trying to divide some number by zero or that a matrix can not be inverted. However, some programs keep on calmly computing things, and sometimes deliver crazy values. Hence, one should always have a good look at what the end results are, and make sure that these make sense. A common rule is that when one gets a parameter value with an associated standard error which is more than a million times the parameter, one has tried to estimate an *unidentified parameter*, which by definition can take any value.

Sometimes people ask which programs I use or can recommend, and I must admit I have no clue, as I have experience only with the program(s) I use myself. There are many journals which publish software reviews, and there is lively discussion and program exchange on the web, and I would recommend anyone to have a look there.

Diagnostics

When the model has been specified and the parameters have been estimated, it is time to diagnose if the model makes any sense. It would be optimal if one could see if the model somehow adequately reflects the DGP, but as this is unknown one has to resort to studying the properties of the model, and often mainly of its estimated error term. Indeed, if the starting-point is that ε_i is distributed as normal with mean zero and common variance σ^2, one can see whether this holds approximately for the estimated errors. In a sense, one can view this as trying to find a model for the estimated errors. If one succeeds in that, the original model was not adequately specified as there is some additional information in the error term that was missed in the first round.

There are many diagnostic measures around, and academic studies on these measures usually start with the phrase "testing for..." For these tests the same situation holds as for estimation methods – that is, that academics design new measures and try to see whether the new ones are better than the old ones in simulations. This leads to many publications on tests, and in turn to a dismissal of old and less useful ones. For example, the famous Durbin–Watson test, which was one of the first tests around and marked the beginning of an era of testing econometric models, appears to be useful only in very exceptional situations and hence is not much seen in use today. All commercial computer programs deliver these test values, but in most instances it is unclear what to do with them.

There are two main types of tests. The first type aims to provide an overall picture by judging whether the model is well specified or not. In fact, it aims to indicate whether something is wrong without telling what. This is usually called a *portmanteau test* or a *model specification test*. The conclusion from these tests is either that the model is not bad, or that it is, with some degree of confidence. In the first instance, one can start using the model, in the second, one is uncertain about what to do next. In that case, one may decide to use the second type of diagnostic tests concerning specific aspects of the error term, and they tell you how perhaps to modify the model. Examples of such tests are tests for normality of the estimated error observations; for linearity of the relation between y_i and x_i against, for example, a relation between y_i and x_i^2; tests for residual correlation; and tests for common variance.

Methods to diagnose various different possible deficiencies can be constructed using three principles. In some cases the resultant tests are the same, but in other cases one might get completely different results. If one is willing to formally compare two models, where one is the model one started with and the other is the model which would be adequate if the first one is not, then one considers a *Likelihood Ratio (LR) test*. This phrase already suggests that one compares the likelihood of the data given the two models. The other two ideas are the *Lagrange Multiplier (LM) principle* and the *Wald method*. In some cases, it is more convenient to use the LR method, and in others the Wald or LM method, and this choice is often guided by the ease of computing parameter estimates.

So far, the diagnostic measures have mainly considered the properties of the estimated errors. However, these measures can also be used to gain degrees of freedom by deleting *redundant variables* from the model. Redundant variables are those variables that do not seem to contribute to the model in a relevant way.

Sometimes it is useful to have a single measure of the overall quality of the model. This measure of the fit is often taken to be the *coefficient of determination* or *R-squared*. This measure is constructed to lie between 0 and 1, where 1 is good and 0 is bad. A single focus on fit is viewed as too narrow, and hence in practice one tends to evaluate the model performance not only on in-sample fit, but also on out-of-sample forecasts. Obviously, out-of-sample R-squared measures are typically worse than in-sample. OLS tries to find those $\hat{\beta}_1$ and $\hat{\beta}_2$ parameters which maximize the in-sample fit. As this is most likely not the case for previously unseen data, the out-of-sample fit is worse. This is not a problem, although of course the differences should not be too large. If that happens, one is usually considering an out-of-sample set of observations which does not match with the model. For example, in a time series context, a structural break caused by unforeseen institutional events might occur in the forecasting sample.

Modifications

Once diagnostic tests indicate that the first-guess model is somehow misspecified, one needs to improve it. The main reason for doing so is that when this model lacks important variables or makes erroneous assumptions, one can use whatever fancy estimator one likes, but in many cases the end result does not make sense.

A first modification strategy assumes that in the case of misspecification, one might modify the estimator for the key parameters, which appear in the model part which is well specified, and in particular the expressions for the associated standard errors. An example concerns the HAC estimator, where "HAC" means *heteroskedasticity and autocorrelation consistent*.

A second strategy builds on the diagnostic test and examines if a new model can be proposed. For example, take again

$$y_t = \beta_1 + \beta_2 x_t + u_t, \qquad (3.21)$$

and suppose one finds that there is strong first order autocorrelation in the estimated errors, that is,

$$u_t = \rho_1 u_{t-1} + \varepsilon_t. \qquad (3.22)$$

Instead of using HAC estimators for β_2, one can also combine the two expressions into a new model. When

$$\rho_1 y_{t-1} = \rho_1 \beta_1 + \rho_1 \beta_2 x_{t-1} + \rho_1 u_{t-1} \qquad (3.23)$$

is subtracted from (3.21), one has

$$y_t = \rho_1 y_{t-1} + (1 - \rho_1)\beta_1 + \beta_2 x_t - \rho_1 \beta_2 x_{t-1} + \varepsilon_t, \quad (3.24)$$

which is called an *autoregressive distributed lag (ADL) model.*
This model is a restricted version of

$$y_t = \alpha_1 + \alpha_2 y_{t-1} + \alpha_3 x_t + \alpha_4 x_{t-1} + \varepsilon_t, \qquad (3.25)$$

where imposing $\alpha_4 = -\alpha_1 \alpha_3$ leads to (3.24). The model in
(3.25) can also be written as

$$
\begin{aligned}
y_t - y_{t-1} &= \alpha_1 + \alpha_3 (x_t - x_{t-1}) \\
&\quad + (\alpha_2 - 1)\left(y_{t-1} - \frac{\alpha_3 + \alpha_4}{1 - \alpha_2} x_{t-1} \right) + \varepsilon_t, \quad (3.26)
\end{aligned}
$$

which is usually called an *equilibrium correction model (ECM).*
In particular this last expression is often used in econometric
modeling of time series data, as it separates immediate effects of x on y, by the increment variable $x_t - x_{t-1}$, from the
so-called equilibrium-type effects through the linear combination of past levels, that is,

$$y_{t-1} - \frac{\alpha_3 + \alpha_4}{1 - \alpha_2} x_{t-1}.$$

This elegant model is also the working vehicle if the time
series are trending like the model in (3.17), while they seem
to have the same trend. This last notion is called *common
trends* or *cointegration.*

Answering practical questions

The final issue in econometric modeling amounts of course
to answering the question with which it all started. When

the relevant model is found to adequately summarize the data, it is time to get back to the question. This question may have been rather precise, like **"is the price elasticity of ketchup equal to -2?"** but in many cases it is not and the model and the econometrician have to work together. Remember, though, that whatever the question was, one can answer only in terms of numbers or statements surrounded by confidence regions.

Some practical questions can get answered with a "yes" or a "no" (that is, approximately "yes" or "no") by looking at one or more parameter estimates. Consider the question **"do the levels of NYSE stock returns have an effect on the levels of Amsterdam stock returns the next day?"** If one has collected daily data for the last ten years, say, and one has considered a, most likely HAC corrected, regression model for y_t, then the answer depends on the value of $\hat{\beta}_2$ and its associated standard error. If the value of zero is within a certain confidence interval, then there is not such an effect.

In other cases, the focus is on out-of-sample forecasting. The practical questions in these instances usually are quite clear, like **"give five-year ahead forecasts for our country's real GDP."** Such forecasting exercises can also be used to examine the outcomes of various scenarios. The question could then be **"how does our GDP look like in five years from now, when tax rates decrease with p per cent and interest rate levels with q per cent?"** Naturally, the model should then include that real GDP somehow depends on tax rates and interest rates. One can then change values of p and q, in order to see what can happen in the future. Of course, one has to check that tax rates and interest rates might be affected by past GDP as well, as in that case one needs to have a *multiple-equation model* containing three models with GDP, tax rates, and interest rates on the left-hand side.

Finally, if the model is meant to be applied on future occasions, too, it can be useful to keep a track record of the model's past forecasting performance. How well did it do in that period, or for this sample? This can be quite informative as one then learns about systematic deficiencies and omissions. To my knowledge, this is rarely done, unfortunately.

To conclude this chapter, I should say a few words about the use of the model by someone who did not develop it. As mentioned before, it is strongly recommended for econometricians to state as clearly as possible how they translated the question into the model, and which data were used. Still, it is likely that the end user of the model will not grasp the full details of this process or (which happens more often) is not interested in it. One should then be aware that it is quite likely that the end user will strip away all subtleties in your text and analysis, and will just blindly work on the final numbers. Indeed, if a manager needs a forecast in order to know whether a new factory should be built or not, s/he will not be happy with an econometrician's statement like **"expected sales will be 10 plus or minus 5 with great confidence."** He or she will ask **"Well, it is 10 or not?"** as **"with 10 I will build this factory, but if**

it is 5 I will not." It is really rather difficult to say what an econometrician should do in such a case, as one would be inclined to overshoot the confidence if managers persistently ask for it. However, one should better do not provide suggested confidence, and stick with the first obtained result with uncertainty.

CHAPTER FOUR

Seven case studies

This chapter contains a brief discussion of seven empirical questions that have been analyzed using econometric models. As will become clear, these models are not straightforward regression models, but in one way or another they all amount to extensions. This is done on purpose to show how econometricians come up with new models whenever relevant. The discussion cannot follow the studies literally, but merely suggests topics which are of interest to econometricians and which involve a combination of a practical question, data and a model. The papers themselves contain much more detail, and the summaries here are only sketches of what is in them. The main focus is on the research question, on the data, and on the model used to answer the questions. There is almost no discussion of related literature as this can be found in the references cited in the papers. There are two macroeconomic studies, two marketing studies, one financial study, one on politics, and one on temperatures. These last two are included to indicate that other research areas can also consider econometric models to answer their questions.

Convergence between rich and poor countries

The question of whether poor and rich countries display convergence in *per capita* income levels has been a topic of much recent concern in applied economics and econometrics. Indeed, it is hoped that development programs and increased levels of information flows and international trade might have a spin-off on economic growth in poorer countries such that their output and income levels increase *per capita*. Of course, such programs likely benefit rich countries too, but perhaps with smaller increases, and hence countries may show convergence in the longer run. Hobijn and Franses (2000) aim to contribute to the literature and to the available knowledge by trying to answer the question **"Do countries converge in *per capita* GDP?"**

The first issue is of course how one should define "convergence." This definition heavily depends on how one characterizes the trend in *per capita* GDP variables. Denote the log *per capita* GDP of country i as $y_{i,t}, t = 1, 2, \ldots, T$. Without further testing or diagnostics, Hobijn and Franses (2000) assume that this variable can be described by a model as in (3.17). This says that log GDP has a trend, and also that there is more uncertainty about future values of GDP than would be the case for the model in (3.18). The relevant academic literature suggests two definitions of convergence. Suppose one has log GDP *per capita* levels of two countries, denoted by $y_{i,t}$ and $y_{j,t}$, and consider the disparity variable $y_{i,t} - y_{j,t}$. Countries i and j are said to display *asymptotically perfect convergence* if

$$y_{i,t} - y_{j,t} = \beta_1 + \beta_2 t + u_t, \tag{4.1}$$

where the error term can be described by, for example,

$$u_t = \rho_1 u_{t-1} + \varepsilon_t, \tag{4.2}$$

under the conditions that $\beta_1 = 0$, $\beta_2 = 0$ and $\rho_1 < 1$. In words this means that $y_{i,t} - y_{j,t}$ has mean zero and no trend, while it may have some dynamic evolution over time. A slightly weaker variant of this definition is *asymptotically relative convergence*, in which case $y_{i,t} - y_{j,t}$ can be described by the same equations, but now β_1 does not have to be zero. In words this means that two countries show a nonzero difference in their growth paths, but they do not diverge.

Once convergence has been defined, one can have a look at possible data, where in this case one may assume that GDP is approximately properly measured. Again it turns out that the question needs further refining, as one needs to decide on the relevant countries. As the issue of international convergence usually involves comparing rich and poor countries, one needs to consider data on many countries in the world. Luckily, there are the so-called Penn World Tables (see Summers and Heston, 1991) and various updates, and these contain annual data on a variety of variables for about each country in the world.

Having access to so many data raises the question of how one can evaluate convergence for all possible pairs of countries, and how one should then report on all these results. One way to solve this might be to create *clusters of countries* within which the countries show convergence and across which there is convergence. Hobijn and Franses (2000) develop a method for that. The main focus of that test is that one wants to examine whether the conditions $\beta_1 = 0$, $\beta_2 = 0$ and $\rho_1 < 1$ hold for two or more countries at the same time. Next, one can see how many countries are in how many clusters. Suppose one found just a single cluster, then one can say that all countries converge. When one found that all countries are in their own cluster, one can say that there is no convergence at all.

The first line in table 4.1 gives the main results for asymptotic relative convergence. There are 116 countries involved in the analysis of real GDP *per capita*, as for several countries there were not enough data. It is found that there are 68 clusters, which obviously is quite large and perhaps a disappointing number. The size of the largest cluster is five countries. This finding suggests that there is not much convergence going on, and hence the answer to the question seems to be "no." It is a little difficult to say whether there is no convergence with some degree of confidence, which is caused by the use of many statistical tests needed to form the clusters. One way to get some confidence in the overall

Table 4.1. *Clusters of countries for various indicators of living standards[a]*

Indicator	Countries	Clusters	Size of largest cluster
Real GDP *per capita*	116	68	5
Life expectancy	155	103	4
Infant mortality	150	95	5
Daily calorie supply	160	67	7
Daily protein supply	159	62	6

Note:
[a] This table is based on table 4.3 from Hobijn and Franses (2001).

outcome is to redo the whole analysis while allowing for various significance levels. Upon doing that, Hobijn and Franses (2000) find that the answer stays "no."

One may now wonder whether perhaps there is not much convergence in GDP, but maybe there is in other indicators. Indeed, GDP mainly measures income, but it is perhaps not informative for living standard indicators like life expectancy and infant mortality. To see whether this is the case, Hobijn and Franses (2001) seek to answer the question **"Do countries converge in living standards?"** Again the Penn World Tables are used, and owing to differences in data quality there are different numbers of countries involved in the analysis. From the second panel of table 4.1, one can see that the convergence results for life expectancy, infant mortality, daily calorie supply, and daily protein supply are qualitatively similar to those of GDP – that is, there is not much evidence of world-wide convergence.

Direct mail target selection

The previous example study had a clear-cut purpose, and it was also pretty clear which data one could and should use. This is not always the case, and in fact it may sometimes be rather complicated. An example is the selection of targets (that is, individuals) for direct mailings (see Donkers *et al.*, 2001). Imagine a charitable organization which sends letters to prospective donors with the invitation to donate to charity. An important question is now **"who shall receive a letter?"** This is a pretty general question, but in practice it is rather difficult to answer. First of all, one needs to have an idea of what the organization aims to achieve. It can be profits, it can be donation size, but it can also be building up a long-term relationship. Secondly, the organization can evaluate the success of their mailing strategy only for those individuals who do get a letter. Indeed, anyone who does not receive such a letter will not respond and donate. The list of those who do get a letter is usually based on their past behavior. For example, the charitable organization collects data on (1) the average donation of individuals in previous rounds of mailings, on (2) the number of times individuals have responded in the past, and on (3) whether they responded to the most recent mailing. Hence, there is a possibility here that quite an unbalanced data set gets created, in the sense that for all individuals all past information is not available. This clearly illustrates the notion of *sample selection*. An analysis of those individuals who did donate, while neglecting the fact that they do not constitute a random sample, gives flawed outcomes.

Part of the analysis in Donkers *et al.* (2001) concerns the question **"what characterizes individuals who did donate to charity?"** To be able to answer this question, one can analyze a sample of all individuals who received a mailing. For those individuals one can observe whether they responded to the mailing by donating (so, "yes" or "no response") and the amount of money they donated if they did so. Hence, the monetary value of donation is zero for those who did not donate. In econometrics jargon, it is said that the donation size is a *censored variable*. Letting y_i denote the variable of interest, which is the donated amount, and letting r_i denote whether an individual responded or not, one can think of the following model for donation, where I use only a single explanatory variable x_i for notational convenience. First, one can specify a probit model for r_i as in (3.16), where the probability of response is a function of x_i.

Next, one can specify a regression model for y_i where $r_i = 1$ while it is assumed that $y_i = 0$ if $r_i = 0$. This model is called a *tobit model*, and it is frequently used in econometrics. The key issue of this model is that it zooms in on the relation between y_i and x_i while correcting for the possibility that y_i is censored. Hence, the mechanism that generated the missing data on y_i is also modeled. A further aspect of the model is that it can permit the effects of the explanatory variable to differ across the two equations. In words, it allows, for

Table 4.2. *Estimation results for a model consisting of an equation for response and one for gift size[a]*

Variable	Response equation	Gift size equation
Average donation	−0.157 (0.029)	0.897 (0.010)
Number of mailings responded to in the past	1.544 (0.107)	0.202 (0.039)
Response to previous mailing (yes = 1)	−0.069 (0.043)	−0.038 (0.021)

Note:
[a] This table is based on table 4.1 from Donkers *et al.* (2001), version 2. The numbers in parentheses are standard errors.

example, for the possibility that people who donated large amounts may donate infrequently, while once they donate they will donate a lot.

Among other things, Donkers *et al.* (2001) apply this model to a random sample of 900 donors to a Dutch charitable organization, and an excerpt of their results is given in table 4.2. This table shows the parameter estimates for three explanatory variables on response and on gift size. The numbers in parentheses are their associated standard errors and these indicate that most parameters are significant at the 5 per cent level. What is evident from the estimation results in table 4.2 is that the size and sometimes the sign of the parameters suggests that it was wise to allow for different effects of explanatory variables across the two model equations. And, as conjectured above, the effect of average donation is indeed negative in the response part of the model, while it is positive in the donation part.

How can one use these estimation results for future targeting? One simple strategy would be to take all individuals in the database, and compute the probability of response and the subsequent donation given response. Hence, one can compute the expected gift size for each individual in the database. Next, these can be ranked and one may decide to send mailings in the next round only to those individuals who are ranked highest, as is often done in practice. A major complication here, however, is that the next round sample is not random any more. Donkers *et al.* (2001) provide a solution to this problem.

Automatic trading

The previous two examples did not rely heavily on economic theory, so perhaps it is nice to have one now. A practical question that is of interest in empirical finance is **"does the introduction of automatic trading systems reduce transaction costs?"** and to get an answer to it one may partially rely on relevant economic theory. To seek an answer to this, at least for a specific case, Taylor *et al.* (2000) consider observations at the minute frequency for futures prices of the FTSE100 index and the spot level of the FTSE100 index. Data were collected before and after the introduction (on October 20, 1997) of an automatic trading system, called SETS. Owing to the costs involved, it was decided to cover a period of about three months with the introduction of SETS in the middle. As the data are available at the minute level, something like over 26,000 observations are available.

The key issue is now how these transaction costs and potential differences over time can be captured in an econometric model, given that transaction costs cannot be observed. Hence, the final econometric model should contain a variable or a parameter which somehow measures the bandwidth of transaction costs. For that purpose, the authors rely on the theoretical *cost-of-carry model*. Staying close to the notation in Taylor *et al.* (2000), I use the following symbols. Denote F_t as the futures price and S_t as the spot price, and r as the risk-free interest rate, δ as the dividend yield on the asset and $T - t$ as the time to future of the contract. The cost-of-carry model says that, under no-arbitrage conditions and no transaction costs,

$$F_t = S_t e^{(r-\delta)(T-t)}. \tag{4.3}$$

Suppose there are proportional transaction costs, denoted by c, then there will be arbitrage activity when

$$\frac{F_t}{S_t} e^{-(r-\delta)(T-t)} \leq 1 - c \tag{4.4}$$

$$\text{or} \quad \frac{F_t}{S_t} e^{-(r-\delta)(T-t)} \geq 1 + c, \tag{4.5}$$

where c is usually small. As such activity may have a delay of d periods, there are arbitrage opportunities at time t when

$$|z_{t-d}| = |\log F_t - \log S_t - (r - \delta)(T - t)| \geq c, \tag{4.6}$$

assuming that c is small such that $\log(1+c)$ is approximately equal to c. This notion will be taken on board in the econometric model.

If there are arbitrage opportunities, then the variable in (4.6) could have predictive value for futures and spot prices. However, the same equation also says that such opportunities are prevalent only above a certain threshold, implying that an effect of z_{t-d} on F_t or S_t is not linear but is present only when z_{t-d} exceeds c. This suggests that a possibly useful model is the multiple-equation model

$$\log F_t - \log F_{t-1} = \beta_{1,f} + \beta_{2,f} z_{t-d} F(z_{t-d}) + \varepsilon_{1,t} \quad (4.7)$$

$$\log S_t - \log S_{t-1} = \beta_{1,s} + \beta_{2,s} z_{t-d} F(z_{t-d}) + \varepsilon_{2,t}, \quad (4.8)$$

where $F(.)$ is a nonlinear function. Given that c is unknown, one may choose to specify this function as

$$F(z_{t-d}; \gamma) = 1 - e^{-\gamma z_{t-d}^2}, \quad (4.9)$$

where γ is positive. When z_{t-d} is large, $F(.)$ gets closer to 1, and when z_{t-d} approaches zero, $F(.)$ does, too. The value of γ determines how fast this transition goes. A small value of γ indicates that the bandwidth of $(-c, +c)$ can be large to give the same $F(.)$ values, which can perhaps be best understood if one makes a graph of the function in (4.9), while a large value of γ suggests a smaller range. Hence, the γ parameter is key to the examination of data before and after the introduction of the automatic trading system.

Table 4.3. *Testing whether transaction costs are different[a]*

Frequency	Delay is 1	Delay is 2
1 minute	0.10	4.00
2 minutes	2.81	3.44

Note:
[a] This table is based on table 4.5 from Taylor *et al.* (2000). The numbers are *t*-test values to see if $\gamma_{after} - \gamma_{before}$ equals zero.

The above model can now be used to see whether the γ parameter has been constant over time. The empirical work concerns finding a suitable value for d and thinking about the optimal sampling level. Taylor *et al.* (2000) report the results for a variety of these values. For one-minute data they find γ values of 0.33 and 0.34 at $d = 1$ and 0.15 and 0.72 at $d = 2$ for before and after the introduction of SETS, respectively. For the two-minute data they get 0.14 and 0.33 at $d = 1$ and 0.22 and 0.99 for $d = 2$, respectively. In all four cases the γ parameter for the second period takes the highest value. In table 4.3, I summarize the *t*-ratios concerning the constancy of γ over time. Clearly, it seems that this hypothesis can be rejected in three of the four situations, as the *t*-values are significant at the 1 per cent level.

In sum, the practical question whether the introduction of an electronic trading system reduces transaction costs gets answered with a "yes." Of course, the study in Taylor *et al.* (2000) amounts to only a single financial market, and hence no generalizing statements can be made. On the other hand, it gives a good example of the interplay between economic theory, a practical question, detailed data, and a well-motivated econometric model.

Forecasting sharp increases in unemployment

The next question concerns a rather old and very challenging issue as it has to do with economic recessions and expansions. Consider the graph in figure 4.1, which gives the time series observations for monthly unemployment for January 1969 to December 1997 for the USA. The data

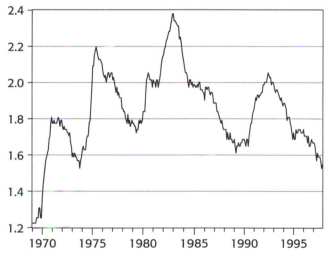

Figure 4.1 *Monthly US total unemployment rate (January 1969 – December 1997, on the horizontal axis), where the data (on the vertical axis) have been transformed by taking natural logs.*

concern the total unemployment rate and they have been seasonally adjusted. The data are transformed by taking the natural logarithm.

The most noticeable feature of the data in this graph is that unemployment has a tendency to go down over long stretches of time, perhaps towards some fixed but unknown natural level, while sometimes the series is lifted upwards. The periods in which unemployment experiences sharp increases are often defined as recessions, and the other periods as expansions. Of course, recession periods usually depend on more than one variable, and not just on unemployment. From figure 4.1 one can also see that increases in unemployment (luckily) last for only a few months to perhaps a year or so, and that the periods in which unemployment has a tendency to go down last much longer. This suggests that the variable displays asymmetric behavior.

What seems to be rather relevant for policy makers is to have some idea when a new period of increasing unemployment has started. Hence, it would be useful to know whether the economy is in a recession or not. Even more, one would want to be able to forecast the first recession observation. So, a practical question would be **"Is it possible to predict sharp increases in monthly unemployment?"**

To answer that question, Franses and Paap (2002) put forward a new econometric model, which is in fact mainly motivated by the graph in figure 4.1. This model rests on the idea that unemployment can be described by a time series model, while the variable once in a while experiences shocks which cause the level of the series to be lifted upwards. This does not always happen, but only under adverse economic conditions. Hence, such conditions would predict that positive increments to unemployment can happen. The main issue here is of course that it is difficult how to define the unobservable "adverse conditions" variable. One way out is to assume that a linear combination of relevant economic variables has predictive value for this unobserved variable. For example, one may believe that when an increase in the oil price plus a decrease in industrial production exceeds some number, such an adverse condition is happening.

A model to describe this kind of features is what is called a censored latent effects autoregressive model (CLEAR) for a time series y_t. An example is

$$y_t = \rho_1 + \rho_2 y_{t-1} + v_t + \varepsilon_t, \qquad (4.10)$$

with $|\rho_2| < 1$ and where $\varepsilon_t \sim N(0, \sigma_u^2)$ and v_t is a censored latent variable (measuring the adverse conditions). One can now choose to consider

$$v_t = \begin{cases} \beta_1 + \beta_2 x_t + u_t & \text{if } \beta_1 + \beta_2 x_t + u_t \geq 0 \\ 0 & \text{if } \beta_1 + \beta_2 x_t + u_t < 0 \end{cases} \qquad (4.11)$$

with $u_t \sim N(0, \sigma_u^2)$, and x_t an explanatory variable (which can also amount to a linear combination of a few variables). This model allows for a time-varying effect of the explanatory variable x_t. The variable v_t is 0 unless $\beta_1 + \beta_2 x_t$ exceeds a threshold level $-u_t$, where u_t is a normal random variable. When the threshold is exceeded, v_t takes a positive value and the downward movement is disrupted by additional positive shocks. By allowing $\sigma_u^2 \neq 0$, Franses and Paap (2002) introduce additional uncertainty as to whether linear combinations of explanatory variables have a positive effect.

Franses and Paap (2002) consider the CLEAR model for the monthly unemployment data in figure 4.1. As x_t variables, they use (in the first but unpublished version of their paper) monthly seasonally adjusted US industrial production, the oil price in dollars deflated by seasonally adjusted US CPI, the Dow Jones index, and the difference between the ten-year and three-month interest rate. The inclusion of all these variables is motivated by economic considerations. The data are obtained from the internet site of the Federal Reserve Bank of St. Louis except for the Dow Jones index, which is taken from Datastream. The last variable might be a good predictor for turning points.

The estimation period is 1969.01–1997.12. Denote y_t as the log of the unemployment rate. As explanatory variables, Franses and Paap (2002) decide to use changes in the real oil price, denoted as Δop_t, the difference between the long-term and short-term interest rate, r_t, returns on the Dow Jones index, Δd_t, and growth in industrial production, Δi_t. Its parameter estimates are

$$\hat{y}_t = \underset{(0.013)}{0.016} + \underset{(0.055)}{0.896} y_{t-1} + \underset{(0.056)}{0.090} y_{t-2} + \max(0, \hat{v}_t) + \hat{\varepsilon}_t,$$

$$(4.12)$$

with

$$\hat{v}_t = \underset{(0.007)}{0.015} - \underset{(0.318)}{1.086}\Delta i_{t-2} - \underset{(0.004)}{0.013}r_{t-10}$$
$$+ \underset{(0.045)}{0.072}\Delta op_{t-10} - \underset{(0.082)}{1.179}\Delta d_{t-7} + u_t, \quad (4.13)$$

where standard errors are given in parentheses. The constructed model is rather parsimonious, as there are only ten parameters in the model for many monthly data.

The coefficients of the explanatory variables in the censored regression (4.13) have the expected signs. Negative growth in industrial production, negative Dow Jones returns and a negative difference between long- and short-term interest rates increase the probability of a positive v_t in (4.12) and hence of a sudden increase in the unemployment level. The same applies to an increase in the real oil price. Owing to the time lags, the model might be used for out-of-sample forecasting, and Franses and Paap (2002) show that the model indeed works well.

Modeling brand choice dynamics

One of the key performance measures in marketing is sales, and in particular when it is taken relative to sales of competitors, that is, market shares. Market share is usually measured over time. The cross-section equivalent of market share is brand choice. A typical data set in marketing concerns measurements over time of households who purchase brands, while the characteristics of all brands are recorded. Examples of these characteristics are the shelf price, an indicator variable whether a brand was on display and an indicator variable whether a brand was featured in a store magazine. Sometimes one also knows characteristics of the households, like household size, income level, purchases of other goods, and so on. The data allow various firms to monitor the effects of their marketing efforts, like pricing or promotion strategies.

An important question that managers might have is whether the marketing efforts have only short-run effects on brand choice – that is whether people switch due to a one-time display, or whether there are also effects in the longer run – that is, people might switch once and for all. Hence, the relevant practical question might be **"are there any long-run effects of marketing efforts on brand choice?"** This seems like an easy question, but answering it is not. A first reason is that individual characteristics, like family size and shopping behavior, are not fully informative for the attitudes, opinions, and experiences which drive brand choice behavior. Hence, one needs somehow to incorporate heterogeneity, which is unobserved.

A second important notion is that a brand choice variable is discrete. If a household can choose between two brands, one can consider the probit model discussed earlier, as two brands can be translated into brand A and not brand A (hence brand B). Where there are more than two brands, one can extend this model to allow for more than two choice options. To model discrete brand choice, one can introduce a *latent variable*, which measures a preference, which in the end results in a choice. An example of a latent variable is utility. Assume that a household perceives utility $U_{j,t}$ if it buys brand j at purchase occasion t, and that this utility depends on an explanatory variable like

$$U_{j,t} = \beta_{1,j} + \beta_2 X_{j,t} + \varepsilon_{j,t}, \qquad (4.14)$$

where $\varepsilon_{j,t}$ is an unobserved error term. The variable $x_{j,t}$ can be the price of brand j at purchase occasion t. Furthermore, assume that this household chooses brand j

$$U_{j,t} > U_{m,t} \text{ for } m \neq j, \qquad (4.15)$$

which says that the utility of brand j exceeds that of all other brands. Obviously, one only observes the actual purchase. Define the variable d_t, with $d_t = j$ if a household buys brand j at purchase occasion t. Given (4.15), one has that

$$\Pr[d_t = j] = \Pr[U_{j,t} > U_{1,t}, \dots, U_{j,t} > U_{J,t}], \quad (4.16)$$

excluding j itself. Naturally, this probability depends on the assumptions about the distribution of $\varepsilon_{j,t}$. One option is that $\varepsilon_{1,t}, \dots, \varepsilon_{J,t}$ are jointly normally distributed, which then results in a *multinomial probit model*.

An important issue is *identification*, which is perhaps easiest understood for a probit model for a two-brand case. When one chooses brand A, then one automatically does not choose brand B. Hence, the choice for A can be driven by, say, the price difference between A and B, and therefore the price levels of A and B are not relevant. The same argument holds for the choice between more than two brands. As brand choice is fully determined by utility differences, defined by (4.16), it is conventional to measure utility relative to some benchmark brand J to identify the model parameters. One therefore considers

$$U_{j,t} - U_{J,t} = \beta_{1,j} - \beta_{1,J} + \beta_2(x_{j,t} - x_{J,t}) + \varepsilon_{j,t} - \varepsilon_{J,t}.$$
(4.17)

Hence, a household chooses brand j if $U_{j,t} - U_{J,t}$ is the maximum of the relative utilities unless all relative utilities are smaller than zero, which corresponds to choosing brand J.

In order to set up a model that permits an analysis of potentially different short-run and long-run effects of $x_{j,t}$, the model in (4.17) needs one further round of refining. Paap and Franses (2000) propose using the equilibrium correction model again, which gives long-run and short-run parameters. They use this model for US data on 3,292 purchases across four brands of salted crackers of 136 households over a period of two years, including brand choice, actual price of the purchased brand and shelf price of other brands, and whether there was a display and/or newspaper feature of the considered brands at the time of purchase.

The parameter estimates in table 4.4 give an insight into the potential of the dynamic model. The price parameters are all about equally large, and the same holds true for the parameter for the feature variable. However, in a model

Table 4.4. *Dynamic effects of marketing instruments on brand choice[a]*

Variable	Static model	Equilibrium correction model
Long-run parameters		
Display	0.05 (0.07)	0.35 (0.16)
Feature	0.27 (0.12)	0.45 (0.24)
Price	−1.81 (0.36)	−1.96 (0.53)
Short-run parameters		
Display		0.08 (0.08)
Feature		0.31 (0.09)
Price		−2.38 (0.33)

Note:
[a] This table is based on table 4.2 from Paap and Franses (2000). The static model is given in (4.17), and the equilibrium correction model is (3.26). The static model assumes that there are no dynamic effects of marketing instruments. The cells contain the parameter estimates and their associated standard errors are given in parentheses.

without dynamics, the effect of display is not significant at the 5 per cent level, while it does seem to have long-run effects (0.35) in the dynamic model. Hence, displays may generate long-run effects.

Two noneconomic illustrations

The above five studies were all concerned with practical economic questions, but many econometric models can also be used for answering noneconomic questions. In this section I will mention two recent ones.

Undecided voters

Eisinga, Franses and Van Dijk (1998) seek to capture the salient features of weekly data on the percentage of undecided voters (see figure 4.2). This graph shows the percentage of individuals who fail to mention a party when they face the question **"which party would you vote for if elections were to be held today?"** The data originate from weekly surveys among about 1,000 individuals in The Netherlands, and there is a total of 921 weekly data points.

As is clear from this graph, undecided voters constitute a substantial part of the respondents, in some periods as large as 35 per cent. Hence, if they all voted for the same party, that party would almost surely win the elections.

As can be seen from the graph in figure 4.2, the time series pattern of this variable is far from constant. There are periods with a tendency for the variable to increase, and there are sharp decreases. The decreases seem to correspond with periods of elections, indicated in the graph by circles, cubes, triangles, and diamonds for National Parliament, European Parliament, Provincial States, and City-Councils, respectively. Hence, it seems that closer to elections people become more aware, and once the election is over they become more undecided, until new elections are coming up, which lead to a sharp decrease. The obvious and relevant question for politicians and their public relations departments is **"do people make up their minds around elections?"** where a relevant second question is whether **"would there be differences across the types of elections?"**

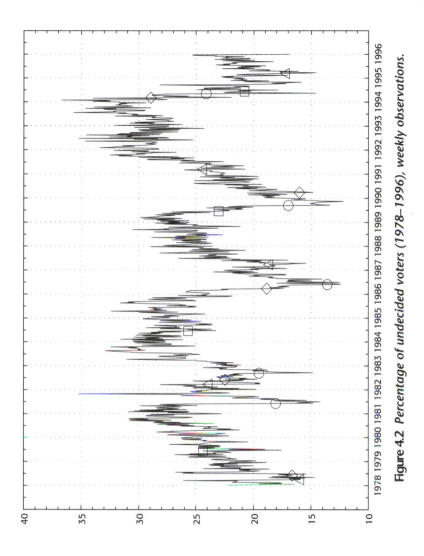

Figure 4.2 *Percentage of undecided voters (1978–1996), weekly observations.*

To be able to answer these questions, Eisinga, Franses and van Dijk (1998) consider a variable t which measures the number of weeks before the next election, and introduce a parameter τ, which should indicate a change after which voters become less undecided. A simple way to describe that is by a model like

$$y_t = \beta_1 + \frac{\beta_2}{1 + e^{-\gamma(t-\tau)}} + \varepsilon_t. \tag{4.18}$$

When γ is large and positive, and t exceeds τ, the average value of y_t approaches $\beta_1 + \beta_2$, while when t is smaller than τ, its average value is β_1. In this particular application, one would expect β_2 to have a negative value, as y_t denotes the percentage of undecided voters. In its bare essence, the model in (4.18) is what is called an *artificial neural network* model.

For the particular question, the model in (4.18) needs to contain four of these switching functions as there are four types of elections. The primary focus is on the estimated value of τ. Eisinga, Franses and van Dijk (1998) report that this threshold parameter is 9 for National Parliament and just 1 for Provincial States elections, among other results. Hence, undecided voters gradually start to make up their minds nine weeks before the national elections.

Forecasting weekly temperatures

Another example of an econometric model for a noneconomic question is the following. Consider the graph in

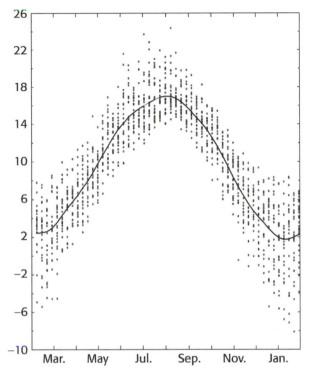

Figure 4.3 *Weekly temperatures (in degrees centigrade) in The Netherlands (1961–1985), plotted against the week of observation, from the first week of February to the last week of January. The straight line measures the weekly average over the years.*

figure 4.3, which contains the 52-weekly average temperatures in The Netherlands for 1961–1985, where the first and the last week may contain more than seven observations. The graph contains dots on imaginary vertical lines, where these lines correspond with weeks. The solid line in the graph is an estimate of the average intra-year pattern. The dots around this line suggest that the spread of temperatures is larger in the winter than in the summer. Hence, the variance is larger by then. What is not clear from the graph is whether these spreads are correlated over time. If that were the case, one would want to have a forecasting model which allowed for time-varying uncertainty around the forecasts, that is, time-varying confidence intervals. In sum, an interesting question here is **"is forecast uncertainty for weekly temperatures constant throughout the year?"**

To answer this question, Franses, Neele and van Dijk (2001) put forward the following model for weekly temperatures y_t

$$y_t = \mu_1 + \mu_2 T_t + \mu_3 T_t^2 + \rho_1 y_{t-1} + \varepsilon_t \tag{4.19}$$

where T_t is $1, 2, \ldots, 52, 1, 2, \ldots, 52, \ldots$, and so on, and where

$$\varepsilon_t \sim N(0, \sigma_t^2), \tag{4.20}$$

with

$$\sigma_t^2 = \omega_1 + \omega_2 T_t + \omega_3 T_t^2 + \alpha \varepsilon_{t-1}^2 + \beta \sigma_{t-1}^2. \tag{4.21}$$

In words, this model makes this week's temperature dependent on a seasonal pattern $\mu_1 + \mu_2 T_t + \mu_3 T_t^2$, and on last week's temperature (y_{t-1}). Next, this model assumes that the variance of the error term is not constant over time (see (4.20)). The way this variance develops over time is given in (4.21), which says that there is a fixed seasonal pattern given by $\omega_1 + \omega_2 T_t + \omega_3 T_t^2$, and that there is dependence

Table 4.5. *Parameter estimates for a GARCH model for weekly temperatures[a]*

Temperature equation		
μ_1	−0.42	(−1.60)
μ_2	6.53	(15.28)
μ_3	−1.30	(−16.40)
ρ_1	0.54	(22.44)
Forecast variance equation		
ω_1	0.35	(1.09)
ω_2	−0.37	(−2.01)
ω_3	0.11	(3.21)
α	0.01	(0.49)
β	0.94	(26.12)

Note:
[a] The model is given in (4.19), (4.20), and (4.21). This table is based on table 4.1 from Franses, Neele and van Dijk (2001). The numbers in parentheses are *t*-values.

on the error in the last week, ε_{t-1}^2, and on the variance in the last week, that is, σ_{t-1}^2. The model in (4.21) is called a *GARCH* model in econometrics jargon, and it is wildly popular in empirical finance (see Engle, 1995, and Franses and van Dijk, 2000).

The estimated model parameters are given in table 4.5. Judging by the values of the *t*-ratios, it is clear that there is indeed seasonality in the variance and that the previous variance has substantial predictive value for this week's variance of the error term. Hence, the question can be answered "negatively," and out-of-sample forecast uncertainty depends on the season and on what happened in the previous weeks.

CHAPTER FIVE

Conclusion

I n this book I have aimed to introduce econometrics in a non-condescending way. Chapter 4 contained some case studies which should indicate that the main ideas in chapters 2 and 3 shine through present-day applied econometrics. I decided to choose some of these studies to suggest that there is a straight line from understanding how to handle the basic regression model to handling regime-switching models and a multinomial probit model, for example. The illustrations were also chosen in order to show that seemingly basic and simple questions sometimes need more involved tools of analysis. The same holds for plumbers and doctors who face apparently trivial leaks or diseases, while the remedies can be quite involved. This should not be seen as a problem, it should be seen as a challenge!

Always take an econometrics course!

A natural question that one can ask is whether one needs all these econometric tools to answer typical questions. The answer to this depends entirely on what one wants to do and say. If one is happy with the answer that two countries converge in output because one observes that two lines seem to approximate each other, then that is fine with me. To me it sounds like the plumber who says that there is a leak and then leaves. In other words, if one wants to get a bit of understanding of how things happen – and more importantly, how much confidence one has in certain statements – then one should definitely take a course in econometrics.

A second reason why one might want to take a class in econometrics is that it allows one to become critical towards what others do. There are many consultancy firms and statistical agencies that make forecasts and tell you that your policy will have such and such an effect. Well, how reliable are their findings? And, which assumptions did they make which may possibly have affected their final conclusions? And, how did they put the practical question, together with any data, into an econometric model? Could their choice for the model possibly have influenced the outcome of their empirical work?

Finally, the possibility of having lots and lots of data, in particular in such areas as finance and marketing, allows one to seek confirmation of prior thoughts or answers to questions by analyzing the data through an econometric model. There is an increasing use of econometric models and in the future this will become even more prevalent.

Econometrics is practice

Econometrics is a highly enjoyable discipline. It allows practitioners to give answers (with some degree of confidence) to practical questions in economics and beyond. The nomenclature and notation may sometimes look daunting, but this is merely a matter of language. Indeed, some textbooks get lost in highlighting technical details and sometimes tend to lose track of what it is really all about.

The best way out seems to be to use many empirical examples to illustrate matters and to clearly separate out the more esoteric (though not necessarily irrelevant!) topics from the down-to-earth practical work. Econometrics is not just theory, it is above all practice.

References

Amemiya, Takeshi (1985), *Advanced Econometrics*, Cambridge MA: Harvard University Press

Bod, Pauline, David Blitz, Philip Hans Franses and Roy Kluitman (2002), An Unbiased Variance Estimator for Overlapping Returns, *Applied Financial Economics*, 12, 155–158

Campbell, John Y., Andrew W. Lo and A. Craig MacKinlay (1997), *The Econometrics of Financial Markets*, Princeton: Princeton University Press

Davidson, Russell and James G. MacKinnon (1993), *Estimation and Inference in Econometrics*, Oxford: Oxford University Press

Den Haan, Wouter J. and Andrew Levin (1997), A Practitioner's Guide to Robust Covariance Matrix Estimation, chapter 12 in *Handbook of Statistics, Volume 15*, 291–341, Amsterdam: North-Holland

Donkers, Bas, Jedid-Jah J. Jonker, Richard Paap and Philip Hans Franses (2001), Modeling Target Selection, *Marketing Science*, third version submitted

Eisinga, Rob, Philip Hans Franses and Dick J.C. van Dijk (1998), Timing of Vote Decision in First and Second Order Dutch Elections 1978–1995: Evidence from Artificial Neural Networks, in Walter R. Mebane, Jr (ed.), *Political Analysis*, Ann Arbor: University of Michigan Press, 117–142

Engle, Robert F. (1995), *ARCH, Selected Readings*, Oxford: Oxford University Press

References

Franses, Philip Hans (1998), *Time Series Models for Business and Economic Forecasting*, 1st edn., Cambridge: Cambridge University Press

(2001), Some Comments on Seasonal Adjustment, *Revista De Economia del Rosario* (Bogota, Colombia), 4, 9–16

Franses, Philip Hans and Dick J.C. van Dijk (2000), *Non-Linear Time Series Models in Empirical Finance*, Cambridge: Cambridge University Press

Franses, Philip Hans, Jack Neele and Dick J.C. van Dijk (2001), Modeling Asymmetric Volatility in Weekly Dutch Temperature Data, *Environmental Modelling and Software*, 16, 131–137

Franses, Philip Hans and Richard Paap (2001), *Quantitative Models in Marketing Research*, Cambridge: Cambridge University Press

(2002), Censored Latent Effects Autoregression, with an Application to US Unemployment, *Journal of Applied Econometrics*, 17, 347–366

Goldberger, Arthur S. (1991), *A Course in Econometrics*, Cambridge MA: Harvard University Press

Granger, Clive W.J. (1994), A Review of Some Recent Textbooks of Econometrics, *Journal of Economic Literature*, 32, 115–122

(1999), *Empirical Modeling in Economics*, Cambridge: Cambridge University Press

Greene, William H. (1999), *Econometric Analysis*, 4th edn., New York: Prentice-Hall

Griffiths, William E., R. Carter Hill and George G. Judge (1993), *Learning and Practicing Econometrics*, New York: Wiley

Gujarati, Damodar N. (1999), *Basic Econometrics*, New York: McGraw-Hill

Hall, Robert (1978), Stochastic Implications of the Life-Cycle Permanent Income Hypothesis: Theory and Evidence, *Journal of Political Economy*, 86, 971–987

Hamilton, James D. (1994), *Time Series Analysis*, Princeton: Princeton University Press

Heij, Christiaan, Paul M. de Boer, Philip Hans Franses, Teun Kloek and Herman K. van Dijk (2002), *Econometrics*, Erasmus University Rotterdam, manuscript

Hendry, David F. (1995), *Dynamic Econometrics*, Oxford: Oxford University Press

Hobijn, Bart and Philip Hans Franses (2000), Asymptotically Perfect and Relative Convergence of Productivity, *Journal of Applied Econometrics*, 15, 59–81

  (2001), Are Living Standards Converging?, *Structural Change and Economic Dynamics*, 12, 171–200

Johnston, Jack and John Dinardo (1996), *Econometric Methods*, New York: McGraw-Hill

Kennedy, Peter (1998), *A Guide to Econometrics*, 4th edn., Oxford: Basil Blackwell

Koop, Gary (2000), *Analysis of Economic Data*, New York: Wiley

Louviere, Jordan, J., David A. Hensher and Joffre D. Swait (2000), *Stated Choice Models; Analysis and Applications*, Cambridge: Cambridge University Press

Morgan, Mary (1990), *History of Econometric Ideas*, Cambridge: Cambridge University Press

  (2002), Models, Stories, and the Economic World, in Uskali Maki (ed.), *Fact and Fiction in Economics*, Cambridge: Cambridge University Press

Paap, Richard (2002), What Are the Advantages of MCMC Based Inference in Latent Variable Models?, *Statistica Neerlandica*, 56, 2–22

Paap, Richard and Philip Hans Franses (2000), A Dynamic Multinomial Probit Model for Brand Choice with Different Long-Run and Short-Run Effects of Marketing Variables, *Journal of Applied Econometrics*, 15, 717–744

Poirier, Dale J. (1995), *Intermediate Statistics and Econometrics: A Comparative Approach*, Cambridge MA: MIT Press

Ramanathan, Ramu (1997), *Introductory Econometrics with Applications*, Fort Worth: Dryden Press

Ruud, Paul A. (2000), *An Introduction to Classical Econometric Theory*, Oxford: Oxford University Press

Samuelson, Paul (1965), Proof that Properly Anticipated Prices Fluctuate Randomly, *Industrial Management Review*, 6, 41–49

Summers, Lawrence H. (1991), The Scientific Illusion in Empirical

Macroeconomics, *Scandinavian Journal of Economics*, 93, 129–148

Summers, R. and A. Heston (1991), The Penn World Table (Mark 5): An Expanded Set of International Comparisons, 1950–1988, *Quarterly Journal of Economics*, 106, 327–368

Taylor, Nick, Dick J.C. van Dijk, Philip Hans Franses and André Lucas (2000), SETS, Arbitrage Activity, and Stock Price Dynamics, *Journal of Banking and Finance*, 24, 1289–1306

Verbeek, Marno (2000), *A Guide to Modern Econometrics*, New York: Wiley

Verhoef, Peter C., Philip Hans Franses and Janny C. Hoekstra (2001), The Impact of Satisfaction and Payment Equity on Cross-Buying: A Dynamic Model for a Multi-Service Provider, *Journal of Retailing*, 77, 359–378

Wansbeek, Tom J. and Michel Wedel (eds.) (1999), *Marketing and Econometrics*, Special Issue of the *Journal of Econometrics*, 89, 1–458

White, Halbert (2000), *Asymptotic Theory for Econometricians*, San Diego: Academic Press

Wooldridge, Jeffrey M. (1999), *Introductory Econometrics*, Southwestern College: Thomson Publishers

Index

Index